TENNIS

MAGIC

© Copyright 2005 Stephen Mallory.
All rights reserved. No part of this publication may be reproduced, stored in a retrieval system, or transmitted, in any form or by any means, electronic, mechanical, photocopying, recording, or otherwise, without the written prior permission of the author.

Note for Librarians: a cataloguing record for this book that includes Dewey Decimal Classification and US Library of Congress numbers is available from the Library and Archives of Canada. The complete cataloguing record can be obtained from their online database at:
www.collectionscanada.ca/amicus/index-e.html
ISBN 1-4120-4202-x

TRAFFORD

Offices in Canada, USA, Ireland and UK

This book was published *on-demand* in cooperation with Trafford Publishing. On-demand publishing is a unique process and service of making a book available for retail sale to the public taking advantage of on-demand manufacturing and Internet marketing. On-demand publishing includes promotions, retail sales, manufacturing, order fulfilment, accounting and collecting royalties on behalf of the author.

Book sales for North America and international:
Trafford Publishing, 6E–2333 Government St.,
Victoria, BC v8t 4p4 CANADA
phone 250 383 6864 (toll-free 1 888 232 4444)
fax 250 383 6804; email to orders@trafford.com

Book sales in Europe:
Trafford Publishing (uk) Ltd., Enterprise House, Wistaston Road Business Centre,
Wistaston Road, Crewe, Cheshire cw2 7rp UNITED KINGDOM
phone 01270 251 396 (local rate 0845 230 9601)
facsimile 01270 254 983; orders.uk@trafford.com

Order online at:
trafford.com/04-2009

10 9 8 7 6 5 4 3 2

TENNIS MAGIC

150 Magic Tricks Designed To Supercharge Your Game!

STEVE MALLORY

To Gayatri Devi Ma, with appreciation and love . . .

ACKNOWLEDGMENTS

First and foremost, my profound gratitude to my editor and friend, Marlene Holland, for her inestimable contribution toward the completion of this project. No words can adequately describe her patience and nonpareil generosity of spirit. But above all I thank her for her propensity and willingness to challenge virtually every aspect of this work, from concept to presentation. Her keen critique and unflinching demand for clarification have indelibly shaped the final result—and always for the better.

Also, my thanks to the thousands of students who over the years have trusted my judgment and ability to help them grow their games. This book could not exist but for our mutual adventuring toward improvements both subtle and profound—and the learning has almost always been mutual. I am honored and humbled by their gracious trust.

My great gratitude as well to those who nurtured me lovingly: My mother, Gloria Mallory—educator, poet and artist; and John and Edna Mack, Thomas and Elizabeth Pollard, and Moses E. Wood, who welcomed me into their hearts and homes.

For early encouragement, Kevin Madera, Dr. Richard Balvin, Peter Burwash, Dr. Mark Henry, Neal Breier, Jr., and Don and Liz Coots. And for their great help in realizing the vision for the cover, Tanya Moler and Jeremiah Fluent.

Finally, to all the mentors who have touched my life personally—or simply served as shining examples of our limitless possibilities—again, a profound thank you.

CONTENTS

Preface ix

PART I – GETTING STARTED   1
    Chapter 1:   The Magic 3

PART II – THE FOUNDATIONS   11
    Chapter 2:   Overview – Stances and Grips 13
    Chapter 3:   Key Concepts 19

PART III – THE ESSENTIAL SHOTS   63
    Chapter 4:   Groundstroke Magic 65
    Chapter 5:   Service Magic 99
    Chapter 6:   Return Of Serve Magic 119
    Chapter 7:   Volley Magic 125
    Chapter 8:   Specialty Shot Magic 149

PART IV – MAXIMIZE YOUR PHYSICAL CAPABILITIES   161
    Chapter 9:   Body Magic 163

PART V – YOUR GREATEST ASSET: YOUR MIND   181
    Chapter 10:   Mental Edge Magic 183

PART VI – EL COMBO GRANDE: Combine Everything You Know—And Everything You're Capable Of Doing—In The Most Effective Way   217
    Chapter 11:   Strategy Magic 219
    Chapter 12:   Tactical Magic 241
    Chapter 13:   Just For Fun – Sayings and Acronyms 255
    Chapter 14:   Commencement – The Mojo Stone 261

Trick Title Index 265

PREFACE

If you're crazy about tennis, one thing's for certain—you're in a crowded club! Legions of fans on every continent share your passion, and with so many reasons to love the game it's easy to understand why. Whether you're seeking a great physical workout, social interaction, competitive opportunities, or a framework for measuring personal achievement, tennis offers all that and more. There's just one teeny wrinkle . . .

- Millions of players around the world are trapped in a vicious cycle as they attempt to learn this wonderful game for a lifetime. It's euphoria/frustration, euphoria/frustration—in a never-ending loop.

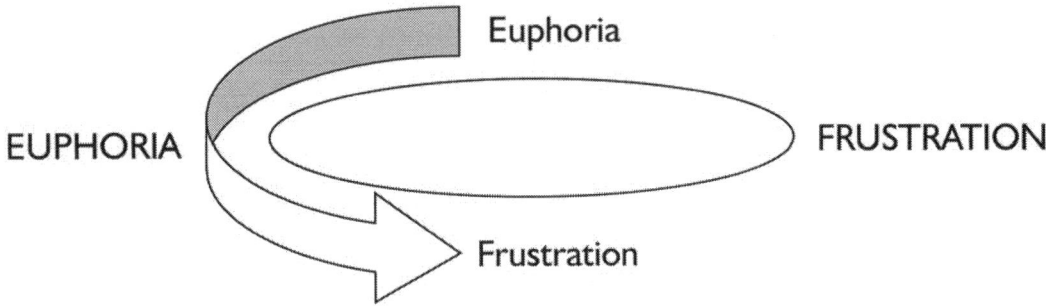

**WELL, "TENNIS MAGIC" IS HERE TO SAY
IT DOESN'T HAVE TO BE THAT WAY!**

- Slow progress and constant frustration *are not* intrinsic parts of the learning curve. It just seems that way because tennis has almost always been taught as a progression of increasingly difficult skills.

Although you *can* learn to play great tennis that way, progress is often tortuously slow, and hard earned advances can vanish mysteriously in the blink of an eye. Obviously, that's an intimidating prospect for any student to face. So if "Big fun—good game—sooner!" is the objective, then a major change is both desperately needed and long overdue.

"Tennis Magic" offers a radical new approach toward achieving that goal:

- Here, everything that has traditionally been taught as a skill is distilled into a simple, easy to learn trick!

And why is that cause for celebration? Well, it's a matter of time and place . . .

- Skills live in a hypothetical, indeterminate future—in the forbidding land of "Maybe Someday."
- Tricks, on the other hand, *live in the present*—in that friendliest of lands, "Right Here, Right Now!"

Needless to say, every student I've had the pleasure of working with through the years has opted for the friendlier destination—and for good reason.

- The payoff is huge. Once you learn a trick, you've got it! Sure, you'll continue to polish it—but in every important aspect, you own it in present time.

OK . . . so much for the riddle of Time and Place: Now we can tackle the Big Question! When beginners watch advanced players in action, their initial reaction is almost always the same: *"How the heck do they do that?"*

A particularly outstanding shot might elicit a specific question such as, "How can I return serve like Andre Agassi or Serena Williams?" or "How can I volley like Justine Henin-Hardenne or Roger Federer?" But whatever the shape or form, those questions are just an abbreviated version of the Big Question. What they really want to know is this:

- "How can I play like a Pro?"

Although the words might look shockingly ambitious on the printed page, don't be intimidated. The query is neither naive, audacious, nor unreasonable. You deserve a fair answer to a fair question, and that's why I wrote this book.

With the help of "Tennis Magic," players around the world are breaking free of their old limitations—and improving their games like never before. So if you're ready to take your game to the next level sooner rather than later, you're in for an exciting ride. In "Part 1 – Getting Started," you'll learn exactly how to use these tricks to help you play like a Pro . . . today!

TENNIS MAGIC

PART I

GETTING STARTED

1
THE MAGIC

Whether you're a lifelong aficionado or a total newbie, the gift is right there, beckoning. Every ball that heads your way is both a challenge *and* an opportunity to respond brilliantly—all rolled up in a fuzzy two-ounce sphere.

Can tennis be a maddeningly frustrating sport? You bet! Can it be incredibly exhilarating? Ditto! Can it also be more fun than you ever dreamed possible? Well, to borrow a phrase from the Stylistics, "You Betcha By Golly, Wow!"

BRING ON THE FUN!

Assuming you can get within hitting range of the ball, there's only one thing standing between you and the kind of tennis you'd like to play—and I'm not talking about the net!

- You either know the correction that will give you the results you want, or you don't!

Sure, physical assets and limitations play a role: Everybody has them, and they are whatever they are. But once you're in position to put your strings on the ball, knowing the correction or solution you need to apply makes all the difference.

- Knowledge is power—and as you learned in the preface, tricks are magic shortcuts for converting your knowledge into results!

Unlike skills, which can seem to vanish temporarily for no apparent reason, *tricks will never desert you!* Regardless of your emotional state, they still perform beautifully—unaffected by the doubts, fears and pesky interior dialogue that often stand in the way of success.

When you use a trick:

- You don't need belief.
- You don't need confidence.
- You don't even need to know how or why the trick works—although inquiring minds love to know!

With or without your belief or conscious approval, a trick just works—and boy, does that make things simple: All you have to do is locate the appropriate trick for whatever you want to accomplish, and then use it when the time comes. Knowing the correction is your boarding pass for the Express Train to Funtown—and the sooner you get on board the more fun you're going to have!

THE TRICKS

Tennis Magic is first and foremost a problem-solving guide. It is not intended to serve as a replacement for the multitude of fine instructional books already in existence, and is certainly not intended to serve as a substitute for personal instruction.

- The mission, rather, is to provide you with a ready arsenal of powerful, practical solutions to your most pressing concerns.

You've got questions, and Tennis Magic has answers—and they're not just theoretical.

- Here, *each answer is a solution*—presented as a powerful, easy to learn trick!

The tricks are dynamic, practical solutions you can use immediately to help you play better tennis *and* have a lot more fun. Armed with these solutions, you'll be able to respond quickly and effectively to virtually any challenge that might pop up on a tennis court.

THE FORMAT

The individual chapters address various aspects of the game—including strokes, body mechanics, strategy, tactics, and ways to achieve and maintain a mental and emotional edge.

The relevant information is then laid out in question and answer form. Each question speaks to a specific issue, and collectively they address the most pertinent and frequently voiced concerns of players everywhere.

MAKING IT HAPPEN

There are two ways you can use this material: You can use it to resolve specific issues, or utilize it as a study guide for overall game improvement.

TO RESOLVE SPECIFIC ISSUES

Find your fix in three easy steps!

1. Find the general heading you're interested in in the main Table of Contents. Then, refer to the Q & A table at the front of that chapter, e.g., Groundstroke Magic, Strategy Magic, Volley Magic, etc.

2. Scan the list of questions for the one that most closely relates to your area of concern.

3. Flip to the corresponding trick/answer to find your solution. Remember: Each trick *is the fix*—the autopilot solution you need!

FOR OVERALL GAME IMPROVEMENT

Pick a chapter that covers an area in which you'd like to see improvement, and then start adding those tricks to your arsenal one by one.

THE FINAL TEST

To merit inclusion here, every trick had to pass a final "Right Here, Right Now!" test.

- It had to deliver the goods flawlessly—right out of the box—regardless of the player's level of experience.

An outrageously high bar? Yes—but an absolutely essential one. Only the tricks that passed with flying colors were awarded the designation "Magic"—and the right to be included in this elite company.

THE BOTTOM LINE

Millions around the world will tell you there's a perfect synonym for tennis: They spell it F–U–N, and that's exactly what it should be! But sadly, the traditional tactic of moving students through a series of increasingly sophisticated skill sets has proven inefficient at best.

Far too often, players feel shackled rather than empowered—and as a result, what should be a delightful journey turns into an uphill battle that's not nearly as much fun as it could be.

The Tennis Magic approach, in contrast, is designed to help you *get the party started now!* With its rock-solid focus on dependable solutions, it provides a practical, user-friendly alternative based on a simple principle:

> **"IT'S THE CORRECTIONS, BABY!"**
>
> Identify the challenge, cross-reference the trick that supplies the correction, and work it for all it's worth.

In the final analysis, that's what "playing like a Pro" is really all about—and once you understand that, you've got a lifetime ticket to the Tennis Fun Zone.

So whether you're a beginner or a seasoned Pro in a temporary slump, start smiling—the future's so bright you're gonna need shades! Whatever your objective might be in terms of game improvement, there are solutions here that will put you on the fast track to success. Every one of these tricks will work the very first time you actually use it—and things only get better from there.

ONE STEP BEYOND

Finally, I'd like to make a suggestion based on my personal experience in sharing these tricks:

- In the Kingdom of Tennis Magic, the more you surrender, the more rapid and enjoyable your progress will be.

So I strongly encourage you to suspend all pre-judgment. Surrender your preconceptions and presumptions, and do your best to approach each trick with a completely open mind.

Above all, allow yourself to see with the eyes of a child, and let innocence be your magic wand.

Speaking of which, once upon a time in a place far, far away—but ever so near as all magic places are—the Loving Spoonful asked the musical question "Do You Believe In Magic?" If you can answer, "Yes," you're already on your way, and the next step is easy. All you have to do is say:

- *"I believe in Magic—and it's time for me to play like a Pro . . . today!"*

Then, on with the journey! Your first stop in the realm of Tennis Magic will be at the Inn of Tricks & Skills. There, you'll get a quick refresher on the difference between learning a trick and acquiring a skill—and how that distinction can change your tennis life forever!

AT THE INN OF TRICKS & SKILLS

Greetings, Traveler, and welcome! We're delighted to have you. As you prepare to begin your journey, remember that the adventure before you is all about realizing your goals in the quickest, most fun way—and that the individual tricks are the means to that end.

TRICKS VERSUS SKILLS

Learning a trick is fast, easy and fun—and empowers you immediately!

- A TRICK lives in the here and now. It's *present tense.*
- A TRICK you learn today can be used today!
- A TRICK works! It's bulletproof—a genie in a bottle that virtually guarantees success.

Skill acquisition, on the other hand, is a whole different can of worms . . .

- Skills live in the hypothetical world of the future. They're *future tense!*
- Consequently, there's always an element of uncertainty: You feel you *might get it* over time—but only with much practice and patience.
- That's an intimidating caveat even for an optimist: And if you have any nagging self-doubts—well, enough said.

Now that you understand the advantages of learning a trick, I hope you'll be inspired to join the many players around the world who have embraced this exciting alternative. And if you're truly ready to enter a brave new world, then with great love and respect I welcome you to the realm of Tennis Magic.

First up is the "Actually" trick—an essential foundation for all the others.

THE "ACTUALLY" TRICK

Q: WHAT'S THE KEY TO MAKING SURE THESE TRICKS ACTUALLY WORK FOR ME?

A: It's simple: When a trick says you need to do something, you need to *actually do it!*

So follow any and all instructions implicitly—regardless of how peculiar they might seem.

- Almost, sorta, kinda . . . none of those shortcuts will do.

With magic tricks, you have to actually follow the recipe for the magic to work. It's like baking a cherry pie: You have to actually put in the cherries, and you have to actually put it in the oven. You can't just *almost* do either one. But if you actually do your part, I guarantee that you'll actually be rewarded with the sweet taste of success. So enjoy, and let the adventure begin!

Tennis Magic

PART II

THE FOUNDATIONS

2
OVERVIEW STANCES & GRIPS

Before you proceed to the tricks, a brief discussion of stances and grips is in order—both for the benefit of less experienced players, as well as to establish a common language.

THE STANCES

Instead of using multiple reference points and complex characterizations, let's stick with simple, common sense descriptions.

When you're inside the court facing the net, with your feet about shoulder width apart and toes pointed forward, your right foot is the one that's closer to the right sideline.

- So when your opponent hits to that side of the court, your right foot is your outside foot. If they hit to your left in that same scenario, your left foot is your outside foot.

Once you adopt those terms it's easy to talk about stances. The *incoming path of the ball* is the key reference point.

- The open stance family relies on positioning your *outside foot* closest to the incoming path of the ball.
- The closed stance family relies on taking your inside leg *across your body* and placing that foot closer to the path of the incoming ball.

The following illustration is a case in point:

Here, Candace has set up for her backhand in an extremely open stance, in that her left (outside) foot is much closer to the path of the incoming ball than her right foot.

In order to change this to a closed stance, she would have to reposition her right foot all the way across her body and plant it in the lower left hand corner of this text box!

Here's a good rule of thumb regarding stances:

- The more open your stance is, the more your hips and belly button will be *facing the net* halfway through your forward swing.
- The more closed your stance is, the more your hips and belly button will be *facing the sideline* halfway through your forward swing.

The following diagram illustrates the full range of stances, from wide open at the top to fully closed at the bottom. Square stance is a tweener, as both feet are equidistant from the path of the ball. Your outside foot (as defined on page 13) is colored gray.

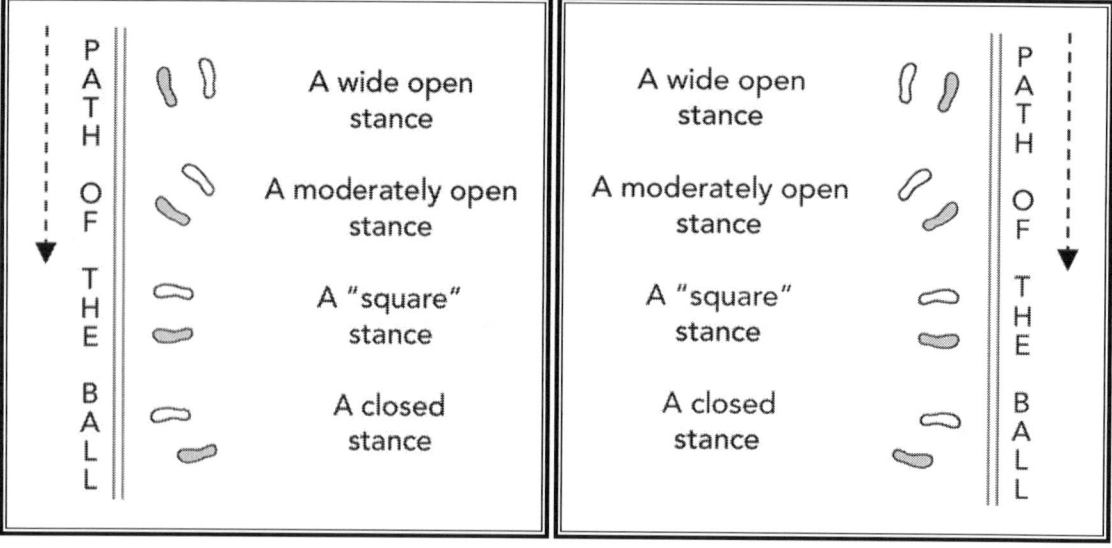

For a wealth of additional information on how the different stances can impact your game, see "Understanding Open and Closed Stance Groundstrokes" at the beginning of Chapter 2: Groundstroke Magic.

THE GRIPS

Here, as in our discussion of stances, less is more. So rather than use several points of reference on the hand and racquet to construct complex descriptions of each grip, let's rely on a very simple descriptor.

- Just center the *palm-side base knuckle* of your index finger on your racket handle as indicated in the diagram below.

Then, for best results, hold the racket with your fingers angled slightly forward toward your strings, rather than wrapped tightly around the handle in a hammer grip.

First, let's look at the grips from a right hander's point of view:

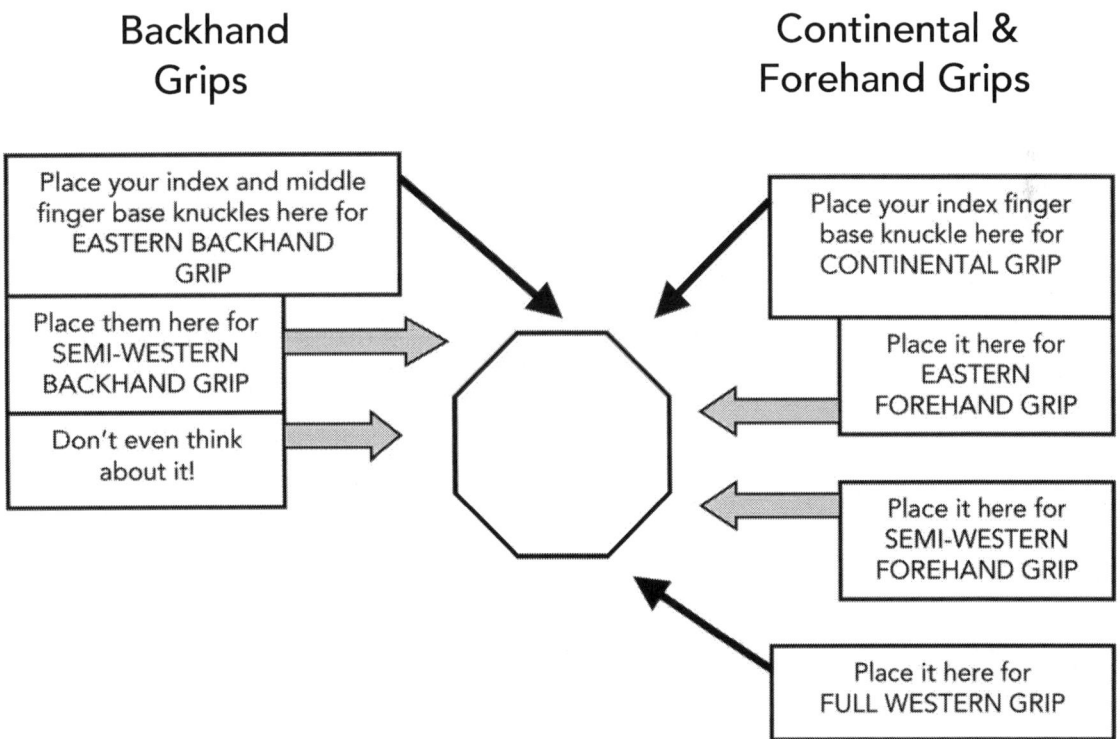

Now, let's look at the same grips from a left hander's point of view.

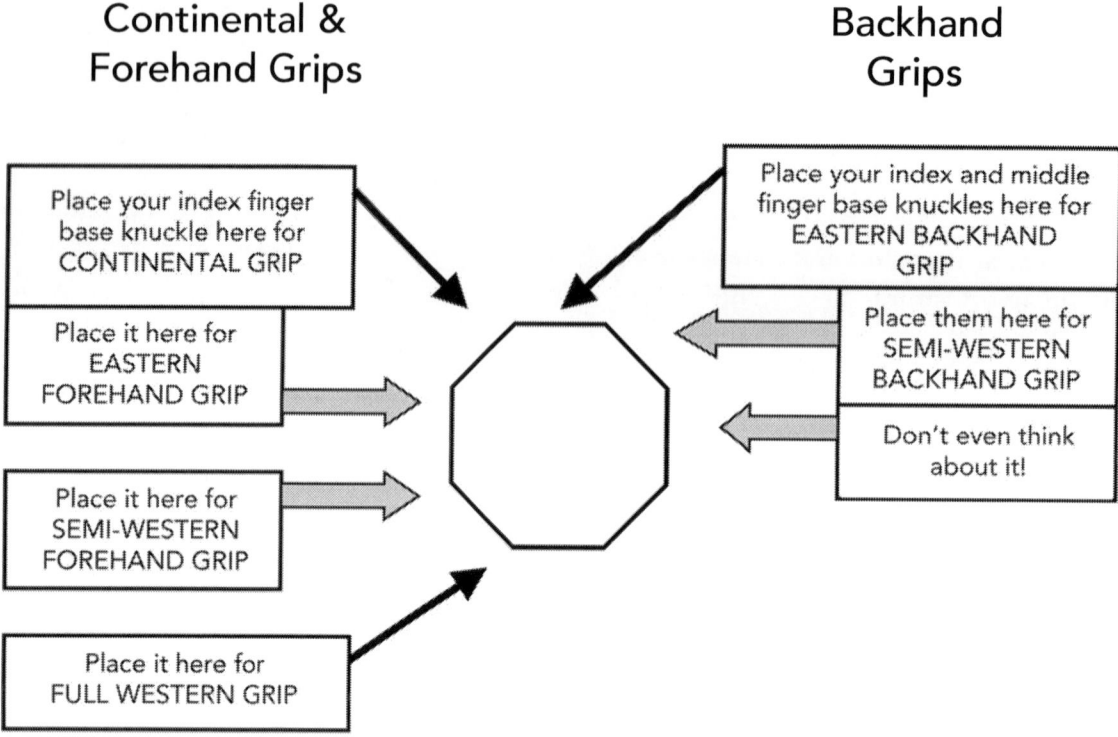

Finally, remember to use the arrows in these diagrams as basic guides, and don't over focus on a millimeter or two one way or the other. Any small variations will fall within the normal range of personal preferential adjustment.

Stances And Grips

3
KEY CONCEPTS

QUESTIONS	TRICKS	
What are the three keys to the castle of tennis?	*Keys To The Castle*	23
I always hear coaches say, "Watch the ball!" Should I just watch the whole thing, or is there a specific part I should focus on?	*The Four Quarters – Part 1: "BIC It!"*	24
This "BIC" concept is totally new to me. Will you refine it just a little bit more?	*The Four Quarters – Part 2*	27
What one key concept can have the biggest impact on the way I think about tennis?	*The Ball Is My Friend*	28
This match is not going well at all—and that's putting it mildly! What should I do first?	*Stop The Bleeding*	30

What revered teaching commandment could be ruining my forehand?	*Obsolete Commandment: Forehand*	31
What revered teaching commandment could be ruining my balance?	*Obsolete Commandment: General Footwork*	33
OK . . . Sock it to me, baby! What's the Revised Commandment?	*Revised Commandment: General Footwork*	34
What are check steps, and how can they help me?	*My Checkered Path*	35
What's the most important prerequisite for controlling my opponent?	*A-B-C Of Tennis*	37
Sometimes it seems like the harder I swing the less pace I get. What's up with that?	*Bag Speed*	38
I hear analysts talk about "staying in the moment." What exactly does that mean, and how can it help me?	*Be Here Now*	39
Sometimes I feel like I'm just hitting away mindlessly. Would you explain the *true* purpose of a rally?	*Bottom Line*	40
When are the two times I should always go to the net?	*Either / Or*	41

Sometimes I think I'm doing everything right technically—but I *still* screw up! Is technique really all that important?	*Faithful Servant*	42
What key concept is indispensable for raising my game to the next level?	*Get My Meaning?*	43
How can I start winning more of those really, really close matches?	*Las Vegas*	44
I know where my racket is supposed to end up on various shots, but I make too many errors when I try to finish that way. What's the fix?	*Let It Finish*	45
My opponent is so tough that I never win even half of the points we play. How can I possibly prevail?	*Magic 44*	46
I let way too many points slip away after I've gained the upper hand. What's going wrong?	*Next.Com*	49
Even when I know something will help me, I sometimes lack the confidence to try it. Is there a trick to help me over that hump?	*Peter Pan*	50
What is the one concept in tennis that's more important than any other?	*Prime Directive*	51
I don't think I'll ever have classic technique. Can I still play like a pro?	*Pro*	52

I think there were about ten different things that went wrong with that shot! So . . . which correction should I address first?	*Sherlock Holmes*	53
I'm having one of those days when I'm mis-hitting everything. How can I find the sweet spot again?	*Super Laser Vision*	54
When should I always surrender?	*Surrender*	55
My opponent has a lot more experience than I do. What's a good equalizer?	*Tried And True*	56
Usually my opponent is the one who's controlling play. How can I turn the tables on them?	*Turnabout*	58
It's sooo hard to remember all the things I'm supposed to do! Poor pitiful me! What shall I do—what *shall* I do!	*Zap The Boogeyman*	59
Is there a trick to help me try harder when things are going poorly?	*Zen Mind*	60

THE "KEYS TO THE CASTLE" TRICK

Q: WHAT ARE THE THREE KEYS TO THE CASTLE OF TENNIS?

A: In order of importance, the keys are:

| PREPARATION | BALANCE | VISUAL CONTACT |

KEY # 1: PREPARATION – Body and Racket

There are two things that have to happen before you can hit the ball:

1. You have to get *your body* within striking distance.
2. You have to get *your racket* into position to put the strings on the ball.

In terms of body prep, the bare minimum is to start moving the second the ball leaves your opponent's strings. If you're in a gambling mood you can even start running *before* they hit the ball—but that's a calculated risk you might want to save for an all-or-nothing poach or a defensive emergency.

Racket preparation is vital, but secondary: It's a non-issue if you don't get within hitting range. Suffice it to say that when it comes to racket prep, sooner is usually better. Nobody ever missed a shot *simply* because they got ready too soon.

KEY # 2: BALANCE – Distance

Balance is a function of distance—which means if your distance is off, you can't possibly have optimal balance just prior to contact. The eternal challenge is to get to the spot where you can most efficiently execute the shot you have in mind—and in that regard effective movement is the key. So always start with a quick burst, and use long steps to cover a long distance. Then, use smaller steps to refine your distance as you move into hitting position.

KEY # 3: VISUAL CONTACT – Watching the Ball

Attention all units: It's absolutely vital that you watch the ball! So why is it third?

- Well, you can watch the ball all you want—but what's the point if you're not close enough to hit it!

24 Tennis Magic

Without preparation and balance you're little better than a spectator—you might as well be sitting in the stands! So first take care of your preparation and balance—and then hone in on the exact part of the ball you've decided to strike. (See the "Four Quarters" and "Super Laser Vision" in this chapter.)

There you have it—the three keys to the castle. Each one is important, but remember, they're a matched set. Any one of them will get you into the outer courtyard—but to gain full entry to the castle, the trick is to use all three!

THE FOUR QUARTERS – Part 1: "BIC IT!"

Q: I ALWAYS HEAR COACHES SAY, "WATCH THE BALL!" SHOULD I JUST WATCH THE WHOLE THING, OR IS THERE A SPECIFIC PART I SHOULD FOCUS ON?

A: There sure is! Each quarter of the ball is a potential target—with unique advantages and disadvantages for getting the results you want. So first you want to pick the right section; and then, focus on it like a hawk.

In order to get a clear idea of what each section has to offer, let's start by dividing the ball into four equal quarters. The letter labels in Fig. 1 apply to a ball located to your right—a righty forehand/lefty backhand.

Figure 1: The Four Quarters

When the ball is located to your right...

Sections A & C comprise the *inside half*, and sections B & D the *outside half*.

- A is the *top inside* quarter of the ball
- B is the *top outside* quarter of the ball

- C is the *bottom inside* quarter of the ball
- D is the *bottom outside* quarter of the ball

Directing the ball around the court is a pretty straightforward proposition: The spot where your strings strike it is what determines the forward direction after contact. Of the four available options, quarter C rules, due to an amazing but true fact:

- You can hit all of your groundies, serves, overheads and volleys using only quarter C as a target!

Few people realize that they can play absolutely top-flight tennis without ever touching the other three quarters—and even fewer understand that it's often a *disadvantage* to use quarters A, B and D.

A and B have the most obvious limitations: They make up the top half of the ball, and when you hit the top half of the ball *it can only go down*. So unless you have a high ball *and* you're close to the net, striking the top half is seldom a realistic option. In most circumstances, quarters C and D will be your only practical options. (See Fig. 2)

Figure 2: The Bottom Half

The bottom inside corner of the ball is always on the side that's closest to your body—whether the ball is to your right or left, a forehand or a backhand.

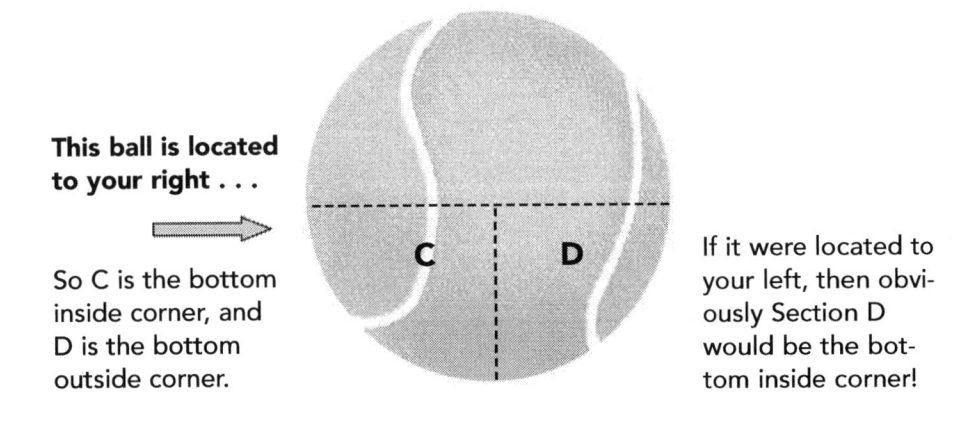

This ball is located to your right . . .

So C is the bottom inside corner, and D is the bottom outside corner.

If it were located to your left, then obviously Section D would be the bottom inside corner!

Anatomically, quarter C is your best choice for consistent results when the ball is located to your right. Hitting quarter D is a lot trickier—because you have to snap your wrist forward to get the strings to the ball ahead of your hand. That adds one more element in motion—and consequently, one more thing that can go wrong!

Here's why:

1. On any given shot, the ball is almost always moving.

2. At the same time, your racket hand is almost always moving.

3. So if you add your wrist to that mix as a third moving part, *you increase your potential risk of error by 50 percent!*

Case closed: When it comes to making tough shots, two's company and three's a crowd.

Now don't get me wrong: An educated wrist can be a real lifesaver. If the ball has penetrated deep into your hitting zone—or is even slightly past you—wristing your strings onto quarter D might be your very best play. You can also brush up around D to make a ball curl back into the court as it travels up the line. But that kind of shot is a true skill shot. The ability to produce it on demand requires great timing and lots of practice, and you can win Wimbledon without ever hitting it once.

What I *am* suggesting is that when you want to go crosscourt, *early trumps wrist!* If you're an artsy, flamboyant player, you can have a world of fun with quarter D—but for most players, your best bet is an early BIC. That simply means hit the Bottom Inside Corner further in front of your body than you would for a straight ahead shot. There's icing on that cake as well: Early contact with quarter C robs your opponent of vital reaction time.

So if consistent, effective results are what you're after, think of quarter D as an exhibition hall for fine art: It's a fun place to visit, but your "Home, Sweet Home" is quarter C. That's your safe haven. So when in doubt, hit the *bottom inside corner:* Just watch the ball like a hawk and then BIC the heck out of it!

THE FOUR QUARTERS – Part 2

Q: THIS "BIC" CONCEPT IS TOTALLY NEW TO ME. WILL YOU REFINE IT JUST A LITTLE BIT MORE?

A: Absolutely. In Part 1 you learned the benefits of working the bottom inside corner—BIC—and how easy it is to do that.

- As long as your racket head and strings are *trailing* your hitting hand when you hit the bottom half of the ball, you'll always strike it somewhere on the Bottom Inside Corner. That's where you'll want to put your strings most of the time.

The ultimate refinement in terms of using that target is to divide the BIC into three discrete sections.

- When the ball in Fig. 3 is located *to your right:*
    - Section 1 of the BIC is closest to your hand
    - Section 2 of the BIC is more toward the center line
    - Section 3 of the BIC is furthest from your hand, and includes the vertical center line

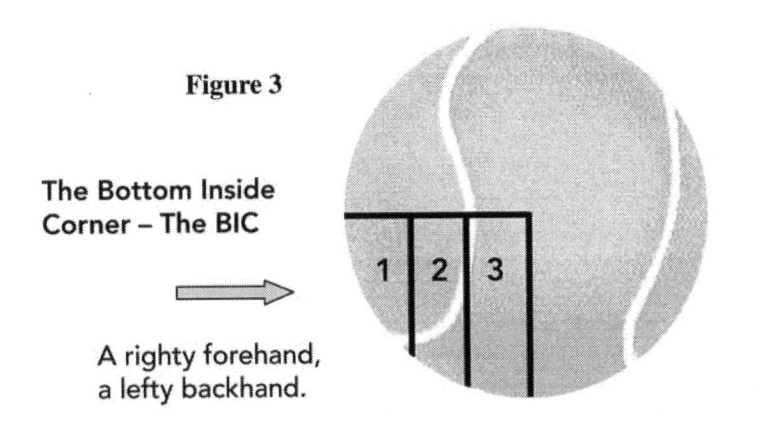

Figure 3

The Bottom Inside Corner – The BIC

A righty forehand, a lefty backhand.

Note: If this ball were located to your *left,* then obviously the Bottom Inside Corner would be as indicated below.

Section 1 is the best target to use when you want to hit the ball sharply inside out. The inside-out forehand is a tactical keystone of modern tennis: A righty targets it to hit the ball to their right-handed opponent's backhand. A Section 1 strike will always drive this ball sharply out in that direction.

Section 2 is located a little farther toward the centerline. It's an excellent all-purpose target: You can use it to either take the ball crosscourt with an early strike, *or* just as easily drive it straight ahead or inside out by striking a little later.

Section 3 is the best target to use for either crosscourt or straight-ahead shots. The further in front of your body you contact the ball, the more sharply crosscourt it will go.

Keep in mind that the vertical dead-center line on the right edge of Section 3 is *the furthest right you can strike the ball with a laid back wrist*—which is a great ally in hitting a solid, consistent shot.

To strike the ball any further to the right than the centerline, you have to flip your wrist forward—and as I discussed in Part 1, wrist shots are skill shots with a higher degree of difficulty. They're definitely makeable—but tougher to control.

That certainly doesn't mean you should never go for a wristy shot. It just means you might want to wait until *the reward is greater than—or at least equal to—the additional risk.*

But never hesitate to follow a strong intuition: Anytime you *really feel* that you need to use your wrist, you probably do! So if the feeling is strong, go for it—and hit a spectacular, jaw dropping winner. Just don't expect to pull it off all the time—especially on a fast court where you have less time to react to the ball.

BIC-ing, in contrast, always provides a rock solid foundation for your strokes. There's practically nothing that can go wrong with it, and you can use it to virtually eliminate repetitive net errors. All in all, it's a powerful concept that will radically simplify the way you think about shot making—and when you look at it that way, what's not to like!

THE "THE BALL IS MY FRIEND" TRICK

Q: WHAT ONE KEY CONCEPT CAN HAVE THE BIGGEST IMPACT ON THE WAY I THINK ABOUT TENNIS?

A: The ball is my friend. The ball is my friend. The ball is my friend. The ball is my friend . . .

We would all do well to write those words on the blackboard at least 1000 times—so that's four down, 996 to go! And if it's a new concept to you, chances are you're probably working a lot harder on court than you need to.

There are two ways you can approach any challenge—you can roll up your sleeves and try to power your way through, or you can relax and look for the most efficient response.

- In tennis, the former approach presumes "The ball is an adversary to be conquered"—whereas the latter presumes "The ball is my friend."

Which approach is better for you? Well, that depends as much on your unique personality as on anything else. One is not necessarily better than the other—they're just two very different ways of viewing and interacting with the world.

Let's look at the adversarial approach first. Thomas Muster did it proud, and in 1996 bludgeoned his way to number one in the world. But that's a tough row to hoe—and if you plan to succeed by overpowering the ball, you'd better be as fit as Thomas was and possess an equally indomitable will to win.

The alternative approach is radically different:

- Rather than trying to make the ball obey you, you can choose to relate to it as a friend!
  - Everything changes once you enter into that partnership. You no longer feel driven to muscle the ball around the court. Instead, you discover you can get what you want just by asking.

OK . . . I hear somebody out there saying, "What a bunch of mumbo-jumbo! You're telling me I can just ask the ball for the results I want and that's gonna work? You can't be serious!"

Hey, if this idea generates a Zen moment of disbelief, that's a good thing. As a matter of fact, "It's all good!" But I digress . . . the reality is you don't need to *force* the ball to do anything!

Let's say you want to hit consistently deep groundies, but you're missing way too many of them long.

- First, go to the chapter "Groundstroke Magic" and locate the pertinent question: "Everything I hit is going long. How can I keep the ball in the court?"
- Then, turn to the answer: The "Big Two, Little Two" trick. Once you've read it, you'll know exactly how to ask the ball to come down in the court.

See how it works? Once you know what you want, you simply ask the ball to cooperate by applying the appropriate trick. It's by far the easiest way to get the job done, *because the ball is your friend, and each and every one of these tricks works!*

THE "STOP THE BLEEDING" TRICK

Q: THIS MATCH IS NOT GOING WELL AT ALL—AND THAT'S PUTTING IT MILDLY! WHAT SHOULD I DO FIRST?

A: If you've been wounded in battle, your first concern should be to find a way to stop the bleeding. But before you can do that, you have to be able to locate the source of the wound! So start by asking yourself the following question:

- "What's the primary source of the damage: Is it self-inflicted, or external?"

INTERNAL DAMAGE CONTROL

If your wounds are self-inflicted, your next move is a no-brainer. Call 911 immediately and stop the bleeding by addressing your unforced errors! (See the "911" trick in Tactical Magic.)

But perhaps it's your opponent's fine play that's the source of the problem. In that case, you need to take a different tack . . .

EXTERNAL DAMAGE CONTROL

- Here the question becomes, "How—exactly—are they kicking my butt?"

The key is to select one glaring thing—the specific shot, tactic or strategy they're using to inflict most of their damage. A quick mental review of the match should illuminate the obvious, and point you right toward a solution as well.

Often, that solution boils down to not giving them any more of whatever it is they're killing you with—whether it's short forehands, overheads, or cracks at your second serve! (See "Knowing What Not To Do" in Strategy Magic.)

- Use the following checklist to help you stay on track as you fight your way back into the match:

    1. Start by addressing the question, "How—*exactly*—are they killing me?"
    2. Decide on *one specific countermeasure*—and then do your best to implement it.
    3. If that plan turns out to be a dud, then move right along to plan B, C, etc.
    4. When you *do* find a solution that works, stay with it!

Finally, reserve judgment of your plan until you feel you've executed it to the best of your ability: Only then can you make an accurate decision as to whether to persist with your tactic or move on to plan B, C, or D. Remember, it's a trial and error process—so just keep on keeping on until you find something that works!

OBSOLETE COMMANDMENT – FOREHAND

Q: WHAT REVERED TEACHING COMMANDMENT COULD BE RUINING MY FOREHAND?

A: "Thou Shall Step Into Thy Forehand!"

As they say in New Jersey, "Fuggedaboudit!" In modern tennis, stepping is strictly an option, and it's a real waste of time to adopt it as your *primary* forehand. If you do, you're just setting yourself up for an arduous de-programming process later.

The story of how that once dominant style lost its throne is a tale of two elements: Physiology and technology. Prior to 1980, closed stance forehands tended to be the norm for hard and grass court play. Players often stepped into their shots to add power or to facilitate moving forward—and even during tough baseline rallies, they usually had sufficient time after contact to unlock their hips in order to recover court position.

Then, fairly suddenly, there were significant advances in racket technology. As powerful graphite rackets began to replace wood in the 1980s, the speed of the game increased dramatically—and anything that hampered court coverage (such as locked hips!) became more and more of a liability.

- Enter Ivan Lendl: A splendid champion who amassed an amazing record of 157 straight weeks at No. 1 from 1985-88. His relentless, punishing groundies set the standard for men's tennis—and exacerbated the defensive liability of the closed stance.

So in a classic case of forced adaptation to the increased speed of the game, more and more hard-courters began to incorporate an open stance—and within a period of just a few years, the closed stance *deep baseline rally forehand* (as a *primary* shot of choice) virtually disappeared from world-class tennis. From that point forward, the open stance *rally* forehand began to dominate play on all surfaces. (See page 67 for a full discussion of the strengths and weaknesses of both familes of stances.)

The phenomenally talented American men of "the class of 1988" epitomized that evolutionary change. Todd Martin, Michael Chang, Mal Washington, Jim Courier, Andre Agassi and Pete Sampras all burst on the pro scene hitting explosive open stance forehands—while Steffi Graf, Jennifer Capriati and Monica Seles exemplified the same trend on the women's tour.

- Their great success was, of course, the result of their extraordinary talent—but the success of that *style* was based on their refusal to accept "Thou Shall Step Into Thy Forehand" as a commandment!

So be equally bold, dear reader, and refuse to be victimized by an outdated chestnut. It's a tremendous disservice for an instructor to program beginners and intermediates that way, but sadly, it still happens—and the net result is that a stroke that should be very easy and natural to learn has instead been made incredibly problematic for thousands of players.

- So if anyone says—over your objection—that you *must* step into your forehand, just run away fast and don't look back!

In closing, let me stress that I am *in no way* denigrating the wonderful strengths of the classic closed stance forehand. (Read about its inherent benefits in "Understanding Open and Closed Stance Groundstrokes" in Groundstroke Magic.) There's absolutely no doubt that closed stance is a great choice when you want to add power and/or move forward into the court. But in sideline-to-sideline rallies, the defensive liability is always there—so in that sense it's more of a specialty choice, like a crosscourt approach shot.

In either instance, if you miscalculate or execute poorly you're probably toast, because it's tough to recover laterally. So be liberated, and feel free to exercise your various options. Yes, stepping into your forehand can be a great choice—but as an *unconditional commandment,* it's a relic of a by-gone era.

OBSOLETE COMMANDMENT – GENERAL FOOTWORK

Q: WHAT REVERED TEACHING COMMANDMENT COULD BE RUINING MY BALANCE?

A: "Move your feet!" It's one of the most over used instructions in tennis—and far too often it's thrown out as a cure-all *in lieu of* a more appropriate correction.

Now don't get me wrong: *It's vital that you get into good hitting position*—and it's true that the *better you move* the better you'll play.

- But it's *not* true that the *more you move* the better you'll play!

The truth is, many players need to actually do *less* with their feet rather than more—so I cringe when I hear instructors and commentators toss it out as a cure-all correction. Even when footwork is *not the root cause* of a particular error, they're quick to spout, "They need to move their feet!" or, "They need to take lots of little steps." Granted, "Move your feet!" might be the perfect advice for *some* players in some instances—but it still might not be the best advice for you.

- That's because doing *too much* from the waist down is just as detrimental as doing too little—and creates just as many problems as it solves!

You'll see abundant evidence of that at tennis facilities around the world, as players routinely miss shots that are well within their capability. And it's all because the "Move your feet!" gang has bullied them into running around like little out of control energizer bunnies.

- Players who are programmed that way fear that if they ever stop running they won't get to the next ball. So naturally, they just never stop running—*even when they should!* (See the "Conquistador" trick in Body Magic; it's a vital concept.)

As a result, they're rarely on balance for their shots, which translates into lots of misses and lots of frustration. And then, in the cruelest of ironies, they're often advised to (you guessed it) "Move your feet!"

That sad scenario is a sentence to life on marbles without the possibility of parole—trapped in a cruel prison where your best tennis is forever just out of reach. But here's some good news: If you're truly tired of matches slip-sliding away, I've got a pardon with your name on it! Just read on for your Revised Commandment—"Tennis Magic" style.

REVISED COMMANDMENT – GENERAL FOOTWORK

Q: OK . . . SOCK IT TO ME, BABY! WHAT'S THE REVISED COMMANDMENT?

A: It's "Quick—Slower—Stabilize!"

As I promised in the preceding section, this Revised Commandment is your official pardon. It's a "Get out of Jail Free" card you can use to ensure that whatever happens from your waist down is a *help* rather than a hindrance.

THE BASICS

Whether you choose to hit with your feet firmly planted on the ground or leap aggressively into your shot, the function of footwork is always the same:

- It's simply a means to achieve the most stable hitting platform that circumstances allow, prior to your final action.

Obviously, the better the jump you get on the ball, the better off you'll be in that regard—so start quick and strong. (See the "Collapse It" trick in Body Magic.) If you need to cover a lot of distance, use long giant strides. Then, you can start to shorten them as you close in on the ball.

HERE'S YOUR RHYTHM SEQUENCE

For a ball that's four or five steps away, use this rhythm to get to it:

- QUICK . . . Quick . . . Slower . . . Slower . . . Stabilize!

For a ball that's closer to you, you can amend that according to the distance you need to cover:

- QUICK . . . Slower . . . Slower . . . Stabilize, or
- QUICK . . . Slower . . . Stabilize, or
- QUICK . . . Stabilize!

I'm sure you've spotted that the key word there is *stabilize*. (See the "Conquistador" trick in Body Magic.) If you do need to take some small adjustment steps to refine your final position, by all means do so: Just don't go crazy with the "Lots of little steps" thing. If you do, you'll wind up smack-dab in Marble Land with no balance at all!

Balance is *truly* a key concept—and in the next trick, "My Checkered Path," you'll learn how to use check steps to stabilize yourself throughout the course of a point. A check step is a pause rather than a stop: So rather than diminishing your level of aggression, it actually enhances it—making you a more dangerous and effective predator!

THE "MY CHECKERED PATH" TRICK

Q: WHAT ARE CHECK STEPS, AND HOW CAN THEY HELP ME?

A: A check step—also called a split step—is a little hop that serves to re-establish balance. It's a defensive precaution that protects you against getting caught with your weight on the wrong foot as your opponent strikes the ball.

The best way to maintain good balance is to take check steps repeatedly throughout a point, starting with return of serve! You can run all you want until your opponent is within striking distance of the ball—but to avoid an unpleasant surprise, it's important to take a little check step just before they make contact. Remember to land with your weight evenly distributed and your feet about shoulder width apart. That tiny crouch sets up your pounce—and from that stance you can easily move in whatever direction you need to go.

HOW TO USE CHECK STEPS DURING A RALLY

- During a baseline rally, time your check step so you touch down just before your opponent hits the ball, because you can't react instantly if you're airborne. Land on the balls of your feet—*that's your crouch*. Then, go find the ball the second it leaves their strings—*that's your pounce!*

HOW TO USE CHECK STEPS
WHEN YOU'RE ALREADY AT THE NET

- Once again, time your check step so you land just before your opponent hits the ball. Then lean forward slightly, unless you're expecting a lob: That way you'll be ready to spring into action as soon as the ball leaves their strings. Now, if you're really feeling spunky, you might want to gamble: In that case, take your normal check step—but then right before they make contact, take off like a tiger toward wherever you expect the ball to go.

HOW TO USE CHECK STEPS ON YOUR WAY TO THE NET

- It's impossible to have a great transition game without using check steps, because if you're running—and your weight happens to be on the wrong foot when your opponent hits their shot—you can easily get passed by a ball that's only a few feet away. Trust me, it's not a pretty sight! So unless they're in so much trouble you don't think they can still fool you, it's wise to take a check step every time their racket starts moving forward, rather than risk just plunging ahead.

That's it! Now you know how to use check steps in every situation. Think of them as the "Get Set" part of "Get Ready, Get Set, Go!" Your mental alertness gets you Ready, but it's your check step that gets you Set—and once you take it, you're definitely "Good to Go." So forget about your checkered past of getting passed—that will all change once you're on the *checkered path to success!*

THE "A-B-C OF TENNIS" TRICK

Q: WHAT'S THE MOST IMPORTANT PREREQUISITE FOR CONTROLLING MY OPPONENT?

A: In tennis, as in all one on one sports, maintaining control is a huge key to success. But before you can effectively control your opponent, you have to be able to control yourself! Without a doubt, the more efficiently you can do that the more effectively you can extend your control across the net.

So let's start with our A-B-C's—which in this case stands for "All 'Bout Control!"

The four areas that define your level of self-control are **Mindset, Attitude, Relaxation** and **Breathing**.

1. MINDSET deals with your degree of determination and commitment. (See the "Do It Anyway" trick in Mental Edge Magic.)

2. ATTITUDE deals with your reaction to events and circumstances as they unfold. (See the "Graph" trick in Mental Edge Magic.)

3. RELAXATION deals with how you respond to mental and physical stress. (See the "Jog It Out" trick in Body Magic.)

4. BREATHING is an indicator that reflects your reaction to stress—both physical and mental. (See the "Breathe Easy" trick in Body Magic.)

As long as you exercise control in those four areas you'll be a formidable opponent indeed, and fortunately, the first two are *100 percent* under your control; there's nothing that can affect them without your consent. And any control you add in the other two areas is a bonus that should lead to even greater success..

So there you have it: The "A–B–C" of tennis. First, control your mindset and attitude—and then your relaxation and breathing. Once you've laid that foundation, it'll be much easier to control your opponent with smart shot selection that reflects your unique individual strengths.

THE "BAG SPEED" TRICK

Q: SOMETIMES IT SEEMS LIKE THE HARDER I SWING THE LESS PACE I GET. WHAT'S UP WITH THAT?

A: The culprit is muscle tension. Anytime you tense up right before you swing you're likely to wind up with even less pace on your shot than you normally get.

- "Bag Speed" is a great, relaxed alternative. It's the fastest swing you can take through an upright paper bag without your racket getting tangled up in it.

To understand bag speed, use this exercise: First, open a large paper grocery bag and stand it up on the ground next to you. Then, grab your racket and take a really fast rip through the bag, aiming for a spot about halfway up the side. What you'll almost always find is that your racket gets a bit tangled with the bag, rather than just knocking it over en route to a natural finish.

Then, re-set the bag and try the same stroke, but at a much more moderate speed. This time you'll notice you can easily topple the bag with one smooth swing, with no entanglement at all.

Now obviously, you'll often need to swing faster than that in a game situation. So the final step is to just gradually increase your swing speed through the bag until you find the briskest swing you can take without feeling any grab.

- That's bag speed: A smooth, powerful, and *highly dependable* swing speed that generates good pace without you having to take a big rip.

Bag speed is brisk, but relaxed—and that makes it a perfect choice when you want to generate reliable power without overhitting. This trick is really all about learning a feeling, and the bag exercise is a great device to help you get a feel for smooth acceleration through the hitting zone.

So if efficient power is what you're looking for, dare to slow down your swing. There isn't a tennis player alive who hasn't at some point tried to hit harder by tightening up and muscling the ball. But as we all know, that shot often winds up in the net—or is last seen headed for Jupiter. Bag speed, in contrast, is a dynamic, easy and effective option: A perfect alternative to *trying too hard!*

THE "BE HERE NOW" TRICK

Q: I HEAR ANALYSTS TALK ABOUT "STAYING IN THE MOMENT." WHAT EXACTLY DOES THAT MEAN, AND HOW CAN IT HELP ME?

A: "Staying in the moment" means giving your full attention to the task at hand. Focused concentration is your best protection against being rushed into errors.

There's an old Chinese proverb that says, "Never try to catch two frogs with one hand." That's a great commentary on the ineffectiveness of a divided mind. You need to pick one frog to have any chance at all, and in tennis the only frog that matters is *the shot you're about to hit*. So focus on it until the ball has completely left your strings, and *never rush to get ready for the next one*. That's right—never!

Here are two important reasons why:

1. Rushing to get ready for your next shot almost always diminishes the quality of the shot you're hitting. That results in your opponent getting an easier ball to work with and a better chance to take control of the point. Good for them, bad for you!

2. Rushing to get ready for your next shot increases your chances of making an error caused by a poor finish. (See the "Finish It" trick in Groundstroke Magic.) Rushing is fool's gold—because if you blow the shot you're hitting, there won't *be* any next shot. You'll just be all dressed up with no place to go: Ouch!

That's why it's so important to completely finish your current shot before starting your preparation for the next one.

- Remember, there's only one ball—and you've got it! So focus on the moment, and "be here now" by finishing *this* before you begin *that*. It's ancient wisdom, and it's 24 karat gold.

Great champions often reminisce about the mystical experience of "being in the Zone," where time slows down and almost everything seems possible. The Zone is an amazing wonderland—but space is definitely limited. So make a priority reservation for an unforgettable visit by staying *in the moment* on every shot. It's a lovely destination indeed, and the quickest way to get there is to "Be *Here* Now!"

THE "BOTTOM LINE" TRICK

Q: SOMETIMES I FEEL LIKE I'M JUST HITTING AWAY MINDLESSLY. WOULD YOU EXPLAIN THE *TRUE* PURPOSE OF A RALLY?

A: It's an all too common misconception that the purpose of a rally is to hit a winner. Close, but no cigar.

- The real purpose of a rally is *to get a short or weak ball that you can use to take control of the point.* If you're not winning your fair share, perhaps you've lost touch with that objective.

The dynamics of a rally are pretty straightforward. The ball goes back and forth until either:

1. Someone volunteers a sitter.
2. Someone hits a good shot that generates a weak response.

Although you *can* get a weak response by blasting the ball right at your opponent, the best way to get one is to make them run for it. That's because the more off-balance they are when they eventually get to the ball, the more likely you are to get a duck in return.

So if you want to win more rallies, either locate the ball far away from your opponent, *or* hit with enough pace to make them scramble. Stick with the purpose, and avoid the trap of going for wacky winners at all the wrong times.

Remember: No player in the history of tennis has ever been able to just bang every rival right off the court—and odds are you're not about to be crowned "King Takethat the First!"

So whenever you're involved in a rally, be patient and stay focused on the true purpose—which is to get a short or weak ball that you can use to take control of the point. When it comes to winning rallies, that's the real bottom line.

THE "EITHER / OR" TRICK

Q: WHEN ARE THE TWO TIMES I SHOULD ALWAYS GO TO THE NET?

A: One of them is obvious—but the other one may surprise you!

1. You should always go to the net *when you hit a very good shot.*
2. You should always go to the net *when you hit an extra bad shot!*

Anytime you hit an exceptionally good shot you're likely to see a weak response, so definitely go to the net in anticipation of an easy volley or overhead. In case number two, however, you're operating from a different motive: It's a tricky tactic you can use to turn a sour lemon of a shot into sweet lemonade.

Let's say your extra bad shot is the result of a mishit. That's seldom a cause for celebration—but at least you know it's going to be a real stinker as soon as it leaves your racket. That's an edge! *You* know how bad it is a fraction of a second before your opponent does.

- So charge the net while they're still in the process of trying to figure out what the heck just happened. It's a great opportunity to use their split second brain lag to your advantage.

Obviously, your stinker *should* give your opponent the edge. But rather than passively accepting that fate, why not be bold! At the very least, you'll provide an annoying distraction—and even if you only reduce their advantage by 10 percent, that's still a good thing. Sooner or later you'll salvage just such a point at a key time—and as we all know, one little swing in momentum like that can change the course of an entire match!

THE "FAITHFUL SERVANT" TRICK

Q: SOMETIMES I THINK I'M DOING EVERYTHING RIGHT TECHNICALLY—BUT I *STILL* SCREW UP! IS TECHNIQUE REALLY ALL THAT IMPORTANT?

A: Technique is strictly a means to an end. It can certainly help you get the results you want—but it's a terrible master!

The term *good technique* is frequently used to describe an efficient and effective way of doing something, and often relates to a beautiful expression of physics in action. But the aesthetics of it is merely icing on the cake.

- The real beauty is that when you're confident a certain action will produce a desired result, you can relax and allocate more attention to tactics and strategy.

That's the upside: Whenever you're on balance and have time to execute, solid technique is an invaluable ally. But how about when you're off balance—pressed for time and out of control?

- In those emergencies, never hesitate to improvise as much as necessary to keep the point going!

Effective results are always *priority number one*—and if you have to color outside the lines to keep the ball inside the lines, then that's exactly what you should do.

- There's a wonderful wisdom quote from the Hawaiian Huna tradition that says, "Effectiveness is the measure of truth." It's a unique way of saying, "If it works for you, by all means use it!"

I'm certainly not suggesting that a game built on wild and crazy strokes is your best bet in the long run, or ignoring the fact that time-honored techniques can serve you admirably. But in an emergency, remember that anything goes—and a wacky whack may be just what the doctor ordered!

In praise of that truth, let's say it together one more time:

- Technique is a fantastic servant—but a terrible master!

So until they start awarding style points in tennis, think of technique as a true and faithful friend—but keep it in proper perspective. It's strictly a means to an end, and never an end in itself.

THE "GET MY MEANING?" TRICK

Q: WHAT KEY CONCEPT IS INDISPENSABLE FOR RAISING MY GAME TO THE NEXT LEVEL?

A: Play with intention! Strike the ball with a clear purpose in mind, so that every shot you hit really means something.

There's a common trait shared by all really tough players—whether they're in a level 3.5 tournament or the finals at Wimbledon. They play with intention, and rarely lapse into mindless patterns of play.

Nothing will get you to the next level faster than that kind of intentionality, so if you're ready to take that leap, start by taking the following pledge. It's a simple statement of your commitment to play with a clear sense of purpose in mind.

- *Whenever possible, I will strike the ball with one of these intentions:*
  - With intent to hit the ball to my opponent's weaker side.
  - With intent to keep the ball above (or below) their power zone.
  - With intent to hit it away from them in order to make them run.

Once you've taken that pledge, all that remains is to apply it whenever balance permits. Intention is a powerful force—and playing with intention will give you a powerful edge!

So regardless of your style or skill level, strike the ball with clear intention: It's a surefire way to elevate your game. Your strong sense of purpose will make you a formidable adversary, and all your shots will say loud and clear, *"Do you get my meaning?"* Shot after shot, your opponent will be forced to come up with an answer. They'll sorely wish they *didn't* get your meaning, but Buddy, Buddy—believe me, they will!

THE "LAS VEGAS" TRICK

Q: HOW CAN I START WINNING MORE OF THOSE REALLY, REALLY CLOSE MATCHES?

A: You can tilt the odds in your favor by consistently doing the little things right. That will give you the same advantage the "house" enjoys at a Las Vegas casino.

In Vegas, the house doesn't care if you win 49 percent of the time—*as long as they win 51 percent of the time!* And in tennis, the math is only slightly different. If you're playing fairly evenly with your opponent in terms of points won (averaging five out of ten), all you need is a little bump to get you over the hump.

Take it from Mother Math. She says:

- *All you have to do is win 56 percent of the points played to ensure victory!* When you do that, there's absolutely no mathematical way you can lose either a set or a tiebreak.

That's because mathematically, your opponent has to win *at least 44.05 percent of the points* to have any possible chance. (See the "Magic 44" trick in this chapter.) Consequently, anything you do to shift percentages even slightly in your favor is in reality, huge!

In closely contested matches, the tried and true keys to success can make all the difference. So never neglect the so-called little things:

- Use check-steps. Be proactive. Keep the ball in front of you. Lean in the direction you want to move, etc., etc., etc . . .

Remember, it's a Vegas math thing—so regardless of how small an edge you might gain, do it anyway! A close match is ultimately a numbers game, and you never know which individual point might boost your total by the mere fraction that guarantees victory. When you take care of the little details, the big picture often takes care of itself—and Vegas is all the proof you need that just a little edge can be money in the bank!

THE "LET IT FINISH" TRICK

Q: I KNOW WHERE MY RACKET IS SUPPOSED TO END UP ON VARIOUS SHOTS, BUT I MAKE TOO MANY ERRORS WHEN I TRY TO FINISH THAT WAY. WHAT'S THE FIX?

A: Just relax and let your racket flow there naturally. *Letting* something happen is intuitive and natural—*making* it happen is a whole different story.

When you let something happen there's no forcing involved. For example, if you're like most people you let your arms swing while you walk, and you do so without any thought or effort. You could *make* your arms swing while you walk—but boy, does that feel weird! It requires conscious muscle contractions, and is anything but natural; as a matter of fact, it's work!

The same analogy applies to a tennis stroke:

- If you work too hard to achieve an ideal finish you'll wind up playing tight. Anytime you consciously contract your muscles you lose some fluidity—and in tennis a tight arm can rob you of both power and accuracy.

Sure, you can bludgeon your shots successfully: Muster, Kafelnikov, and Courier sometimes bludgeoned the ball, and they all rose to number one in the world! But unless you have their willpower and nerves of steel—and can punish the ball even with a tight arm—it's an extremely demanding way to play.

- So if you know where you want your racket to finish, just relax and let it flow there: Let gravity and momentum accomplish the task for you naturally.

The volley, of course, is an exception: A short abbreviated finish can actually add pop to your shot. But for other shots, letting your racket finish on its own is a great way to keep your strokes smooth and fluid. So loosen up and remember that the choice is yours—you can *make it finish* and make it hard on yourself, or you can *let it finish* and let it be easy!

THE "MAGIC 44" TRICK

Q: MY OPPONENT IS SO TOUGH THAT I NEVER WIN EVEN HALF OF THE POINTS WE PLAY. HOW CAN I POSSIBLY PREVAIL?

A: Believe it or not, it's possible to win only 44.05% of the points played and still win the set! So dig in and keep fighting: If you can hold your opponent to 55.95%, you've still got a chance.

HERE'S AN ASTOUNDING FACT!

- The way tennis is scored offers a mind-bending mathematical possibility. In baseball, soccer, basketball, hockey and football, you have to score more points than your opponent to win. But in tennis you can actually score 11.9% *fewer* points than your opponent and still win the match! It's tough—but it can be done!

Admit it: That totally blows your mind—and I bet you're not going to be satisfied until you see the proof. Well, I wish I could provide it for you, but you're just going to have to take my word for it. Not good enough, you say? OK, here it is!

Let's look at the math, game by game, in a fantasy match-up between Serena Williams and John McEnroe. It's a one set match, winner-take-all.

John kicks things off with four aces—his lefty slice serve working to perfection. That gives him a lead of one game to love, and a 4-0 lead in points. He continues to play brilliantly and wins games two through five by the same devastating score. So at the end of the first five games the rout is almost complete: He leads Serena by five games to none, and leads in points 20-0. Believe me, John can smell that bagel! (See Fig. 1)

Fig. 1 (After 5 games)

GAME	1	2	3	4	5	6	7	8	9	10	11	12	Total Pts.	Pct.
J. McEnroe	4	4	4	4	4								20	100%
S. Williams	0	0	0	0	0								0	0%

But wait—always a fighter, Serena digs down deep and battles tenaciously. Every one of the next six games goes to deuce (three points all) before she eventually finds a way to close them out five points to three. So although she still trails in points 30-38, she's now ahead in the set by six games to five! (See Fig. 2)

Fig. 2 (After 11 games)

GAME	1	2	3	4	5	6	7	8	9	10	11	12	Total Pts.	Pct.
J. McEnroe	4	4	4	4	4	3	3	3	3	3	3		38	55.88%
S. Williams	0	0	0	0	0	5	5	5	5	5	5		30	44.12%

Now, teetering on the brink of defeat, John once again finds his early form. He returns serve brilliantly and breaks Serena in the twelfth game four points to none. That boosts his point lead to 42-30.

On they go to the tiebreak, in which they both play their best tennis of the day—and at five all it's anybody's match. Then suddenly, on successive points, Serena charges the net—and with two mighty swinging volleys it's all over! The crowd rises as one in tumultuous applause, and as McEnroe stands stunned with hands on hips, Serena flings her racket fifty feet into the air. In the greatest comeback of her life, she has emerged victorious 7-6 (7-5). It's an amazing win well earned—but what's really amazing is the final tally! (See Fig. 3)

Fig. 3 (All totals)

GAME	1	2	3	4	5	6	7	8	9	10	11	12	TB	Total Pts.	Pct.
J. McEnroe	4	4	4	4	4	3	3	3	3	3	3	4	5	47/84	55.95%
S. Williams	0	0	0	0	0	5	5	5	5	5	5	0	7	37/84	44.05%

- *Serena won just 37 of the 84 points played—only 44.05 percent!* Does she care? Not a bit . . . it still goes in the record books as a big fat "W," baby!

Winning with fewer points is a tough row to hoe—but the math is irrefutable: It *can* be done. So in the words of the great basketball coach Jimmy Valvano, "Don't give up, don't ever give up!" Never, ever, ever.

Now please don't come looking for me, John—*this match was purely hypothetical, and for instructional purposes only!* The smart money says a highly motivated Johnny Mc is a huge favorite in a rematch—*if* Serena decides to give him one!

Nota Bene: Tennis fans were treated to a wonderful example of this trick when Joachim Johansson met Andy Roddick in the 2004 US Open quarterfinals. Joachim was flawless in winning the first two sets 6-4, 6-4, and Andy was equally brilliant in winning the third and fourth sets 6-3, 6-2, with a total of three unforced errors. Yes, three! The final hard-fought set went to Johansson 6-4, which gave him a total of 23 games to Roddick's 24.

But here's the kicker:

- Of the 280 total points played, Roddick won 152 of them (54.3%) while Johansson won only 128, (45.7%). Now, that reads like great news for Andy, but it was also the bad news. Johansson succeeded in eking out just a hair more than the Magic 44% he needed to stay alive!

If Andy had won just *five* more points—*anytime over the course of the five sets*—it would have given him the Magic 56% that guarantees victory. But Joachim scratched and fought and won his Magic 44%—and in so doing, found a way to win the match!

Long story short, this ain't just math, and it ain't just theory: We're talking real life, real world, you're really on your way to the US Open semis here. So fight, fight, fight for the Magic 44%—and *never,* ever, ever give up!

THE "NEXT.COM" TRICK

Q: I LET WAY TOO MANY POINTS SLIP AWAY AFTER I'VE GAINED THE UPPER HAND. WHAT'S GOING WRONG?

A: After you hit your shots, get ready immediately for whatever needs to be done next. Otherwise, your existing advantage can disappear in a flash.

Let's look at a couple of all too familiar examples:

1. You get your opponent in trouble with a superbly constructed series of shots, or maybe you just hit a shot that was better than you intended. If you come right in you'll have a sitting duck put-away—but no, that would be waaay too easy! Instead, you decide to come in late, and get caught in the wrong grip to boot. Hello! You just logged on to *www.missedchance.com*.

2. Your opponent makes an amazing get while you're smugly admiring your "winner." By the time you snap out of it, the point is back to neutral—and *you're* back to that same funky web page!

Believe me, you don't want to spend a lot of time browsing that site—the URL you really want is *www.next.com*. It's quite a unique web page, in that the only thing you'll find there is the following question:

- *"Were you ready for what needed to be done next!"*

So if you lose a point you know you should have won, log on mentally and answer that question. If the answer is "No," then take a second to clear the slate with a positive visualization.

- All-courters: Visualize yourself moving in, ready to volley in continental grip.
- Baseliners: Visualize yourself setting up in plenty of time to rip a groundie into the open court.

Positive visualization always plants seeds in your subconscious mind. Just water them with a little desire and determination and they'll sprout instantly.

Last but not least, don't forget to factor in your opponent's tendencies: Anticipating a drop shot or lob is a key part of being ready. Remember, it's tennis, not golf—there's no *standing and watching* allowed while you've got a racket in your hand. So by all means bookmark *www.next.com* in your Favorites, and be sure to log on regularly. Once you gain the upper hand in a point, that link is your shortcut to victory!

THE "PETER PAN" TRICK

Q: EVEN WHEN I KNOW SOMETHING WILL HELP ME, I SOMETIMES LACK THE CONFIDENCE TO TRY IT. IS THERE A TRICK TO HELP ME OVER THAT HUMP?

A: If you're among the many players who can benefit from greater self-confidence, this trick will get you off to a flying start in the right direction.

In the wonderful fable Peter Pan, Peter so wanted to fly—but no matter what he tried he couldn't get off the ground. Luckily, the magical fairy Tinkerbelle was there to save the day. She told him in just four words what the solution was: She said, "You have to believe!" That was all Peter needed to hear—and from that moment on he was able to fly.

As it was true for Peter, it's true for all of us—until we believe we can fly, we probably can't. But even if you lack the courage of true belief, there's still a way to prevail.

- *Start by pretending!* Simply pretend that you're already a fearless warrior—ready, willing and able to at least make the attempt.

Whatever it is that you want to accomplish, pretend that it's well within your power to do it—because as soon as you start to pretend that way, newfound courage and confidence will course through your veins. Your positive mental attitude will engender greater and greater success—and in no time at all pretending will be replaced by strong, well-founded belief.

So refuse to let lack of confidence hold you back any longer: There's no time like the present for you to take flight. We both know you're ready to play better tennis, and now you know how to do it. The first and most important step is a simple one: You just have to believe!

THE "PRIME DIRECTIVE" TRICK

Q: WHAT IS THE ONE CONCEPT IN TENNIS THAT'S MORE IMPORTANT THAN ANY OTHER?

A: Always hit the ball over the net!

If you're a fan of the series Star Trek, you're already familiar with the phrase, "The Prime Directive." It refers to the one regulation in the Star Fleet Manual that overrides all other considerations. Now, as tennis players we aren't bound by that manual—but we do have a unique Prime Directive of our own.

- In tennis, it's "Always hit the ball over the net!" Anything else we might say about tennis is simply a refinement or elaboration of that injunction.

Sure, it's vitally important to hit the ball into the court as well—but that's still a secondary consideration. As long as you hit the ball over the net you always have *at least a chance of winning the point*—because your opponent might flag a ball that's on its way out, or miss an easy put-away. Hypothetical? Sure, but there's one thing we know for certain. Barring a rule violation by your opponent (such as their racket hitting the net), it's *impossible* for you to win a point unless you clear the net!

So follow the Prime Directive impeccably, and *always* hit the ball over the net. It is—in the immortal words of Commander Spock—a great strategy for seeing to it that you "Live long and prosper!" on the tennis court.

FANTASY CAMP AWARD

For winning by hitting the ball into the net!

YOUR NAME HERE?

Unh-unh . . . Sorry! It just ain't gonna happen!

THE "PRO" TRICK

Q: I DON'T THINK I'LL EVER HAVE CLASSIC TECHNIQUE. CAN I STILL PLAY LIKE A PRO?

A: Absolutely—as long as you follow this pro principle:

- "A seasoned pro takes what's available, when it's available!"

And what exactly does that mean?

- It means whenever a seasoned pro spots an opening or a weakness, they act to take advantage right then—while the getting is good!

Let's look at a few examples of how a weakness can be revealed by either a particular circumstance *or* by court position.

EXPOSURE VIA A PARTICULAR CIRCUMSTANCE

1. A player with a "Nervous Nellie" second serve stands nakedly exposed each time they miss their first serve. So play like a pro by moving in closer to put even more pressure on them—and threaten to return with your stronger shot by over-shifting right or left.
2. A player that uses a full western grip often has a tough time with extremely low balls. So play like a pro by attacking the net when you hit a shot that's going to give them that kind of trouble.

EXPOSURE VIA COURT POSITION

1. A player with a weak overhead is nakedly exposed whenever they're close to the net. So play like a pro by lobbing them—unless you're practically *sure* you can hit a successful passing shot. If you happen to be a charter member of the "Cruel Club," you might even want to bring your opponent in with a drop shot and *then* lob! Now, that's a brutal combination!
2. A player who moves poorly is nakedly exposed whenever they're pulled out wide. So play like a pro by always hitting your next shot to the open court. It's a perfect opportunity to finish them off with location rather than power.

The common thread in all instances is this: *You want to take what's available when it's available!* That's the defining characteristic of a consummate pro, and it doesn't take pretty strokes to play that way. Any dependable shot—however odd it might look—will work just fine. Remember: Effectiveness is the real measure of truth, and results trump form every time.

So never let a lack of classic technique hold you back. Your strokes might be a little unorthodox . . . but so what! If you concentrate on taking advantage of your opportunities, anyone with a real eye for the game will see that *you're the one* who's playing like a pro.

THE "SHERLOCK HOLMES" TRICK

Q: I THINK THERE WERE ABOUT TEN DIFFERENT THINGS THAT WENT WRONG WITH THAT SHOT! SO . . . WHICH CORRECTION SHOULD I ADDRESS FIRST?

A: The trick is to think like Sherlock Holmes: When asked how he reached his brilliant conclusions, his dry response was, *"Never be afraid to suspect the obvious!"*

Let's look at a few examples of how that advice can help you solve your mystery:

EXAMPLE 1 – Perhaps you dumped a traditional underspin volley in the net. If so, suspect the obvious, and use a more beveled, open racket face next time!

- Suspect the obvious! Forget about whether you did or didn't bend your knees—or anything else you might have neglected to do. Address bevel first, and address the other stuff later! More bevel in this instance is the crucial correction, because more bevel—*in and of itself*—would have at least made the shot.

EXAMPLE 2 – If you sail a forehand way past the baseline, check your grip.

- Once again, suspect the obvious! Anytime you use the wrong grip it's tough to get the results you want—even if everything else is fine. So if you find your grip was indeed not what you intended, say to yourself, "Grip error!" and address that first. Grip adjustment is a crucial correction, because your grip—*in and of itself*—can radically affect the length of your shots.

EXAMPLE 3 – If you sail a groundie way past the baseline in spite of being in the correct grip and reasonably on balance, then check your finish.

- Suspect the obvious! If, for example, you're in semi-western grip, then a good finish up by your opposite ear should bring the ball down into the court. Once again, forget about whether you did or didn't bend your knees, blah, blah, blah. Address your finish first! Chances are that a correct finish—*in and of itself*—might have kept the ball in the court.

Those examples should make it obvious (pardon the pun) that picking the best correction is *not* a game of "Twenty Questions."

- Your decision should be based exclusively on *where the ball went when you missed your shot.*

One of the most counter-productive things you can do after a miss is to start spouting every correction you've ever heard, such as "Watch the ball," "Bend your knees," "Get your racket back," ad nauseam! Instead, pick the one key correction that *in and of itself* would have at least made the shot. Suspecting the obvious helped make Sherlock a legend—and it just might do the same for you!

THE "SUPER LASER VISION" TRICK

Q: I'M HAVING ONE OF THOSE DAYS WHEN I'M MISHITTING EVERYTHING. HOW CAN I FIND THE SWEET SPOT AGAIN?

A: You need to focus your vision like a laser beam on the exact section of the ball that you intend to hit.

Coaches disagree on a lot of things—but there's one point of universal agreement: "Watch the ball" is a superb piece of advice for any ball sport. In tennis, however, it's not enough to just watch the whole ball:

- You want to narrow your focus to the particular quarter of the ball you intend to put your strings on. (See "Understanding The Four Quarters" in this chapter.)

So if you're having the kind of day that makes you wonder if you even have a sweet spot, your best bet is to shift into superhero mode. Remember those comic book heroes who have unique special powers? Well, now you're going to join their ranks.

Your personal super power is super laser vision. With it, you can radiate laser beams straight out from your eyes—and zero in on the ball like never before.

Here's how to get the most out of your super power:

Let's say you've made a shot selection, and you're 100 percent sure which quarter of the ball you want to hit. Now's the time to use your super laser vision to burn a hole right in that exact spot.

- Focus on making that part of the ball really sizzle—and then take your strings right to it.

The magic here is in the degree of clarity you achieve when you narrow your visual focus that way. All the extraneous stuff fades into the background: Suddenly, it's just you and the ball.

This trick has a particularly broad application in that you can use it on any kind of shot. Whenever you laser the ball you're much more likely to find the sweet spot—and your increased level of concentration will benefit your entire game. So "Laser on!" like a superhero to get rid of pesky mishits. Once you make a habit of it, don't be surprised if you start burning through your opponents like a laser beam through butter.

THE "SURRENDER" TRICK

Q: WHEN SHOULD I ALWAYS SURRENDER?

A: Anytime you're forced to volley up, surrender to the reality that you're *temporarily on defense*—if only for that one shot.

It's great to maintain an aggressive attitude in your play—but it's equally important to accurately assess shifting conditions. Sure, you may have hit a super approach, and you might be cool and relaxed at ideal volley position. But guess what:

- A great low shot by your opponent changes everything. Suddenly, you're squarely on defense!

Now you're forced to volley up—and if you insist on going for an offensive shot in that situation you can expect to make a lot of errors. It's just too tough a play to make consistently against a low ball and a tough opponent.

- The smart play here is to keep the point going with your best defensive shot. Remember, it's only a temporary surrender. Chances are good that your superior court position will enable you to immediately get back on offense.

Boxing offers a very useful analogy. Occasionally, a fighter who's badly hurt will voluntarily go down on one knee—realizing it's better to swallow their pride and accept a knockdown than stay upright and absorb the next punch. That tactic of *temporary* surrender gives them a full nine seconds to regroup before they have to continue—and can spell the difference between a bad round and a bad *night!*

So never hesitate to buy precious time by opting for a *temporary* surrender. After all, a brief shift to defensive mode is a small price to pay to keep the point going. Yes, it's always good to be aggressive—but a hallmark of *effective aggression* is that it's tempered by prudence. So use this trick wisely to increase the odds that it's *your* hand that gets raised at the final bell!

THE "TRIED AND TRUE" TRICK

Q: MY OPPONENT HAS A LOT MORE EXPERIENCE THAN I DO. WHAT'S A GOOD EQUALIZER?

A: You may not be able to match your opponent's experience, but you can certainly help equalize things with these classic tried and true options. *Great choices produce great results*—and these high percentage plays for defense, offense, and neutral exchanges have passed the test of time with flying colors.

TRIED AND TRUE ON DEFENSE

- If you're pulled wide you'll need time to recover court position. So buy yourself that time with either a lob, a loopy shot, or even a drop shot! Be imaginative, though—you don't want to be predictable when you're under attack.

When your opponent moves in it's usually to your advantage to keep the ball low so they have to volley up. That will greatly increase your chances of at least keeping the point going.

- A more radical alternative is the Berserker option: Sometimes it pays to just wind up and go for a winner against all odds! But if the point is a critical one you can't afford to lose, you might want to go with a conservative, high percentage shot.

TRIED AND TRUE ON OFFENSE

- Whenever you feel you're in good position to strike the ball, focus on locating your shot away from your opponent in order to draw a weak reply. If you're ahead in the score you can naturally afford to take more risks—and if you feel really confident you might want to go for an outright winner.
- Additionally, it's important to come to the net any time you anticipate that your opponent is, or soon will be, in serious trouble—unless there's a truly overriding reason not to do so.

In those cases—such as when the sun is so bad that practically any lob they hit will give you fits—it might make perfect sense to stay back. But otherwise, press on in!

TRIED AND TRUE IN A NEUTRAL SITUATION

In a neutral rally neither player has a discernible advantage—and that balance continues until someone either hits a forcing shot *or* gives up a short ball. So until you have a realistic opportunity to take control, focus on hitting deep to your opponent's weaker side.

- It *is* possible to use a surprise drop shot to take control of a neutral rally, but it better be a good one. Otherwise you're just giving your opponent a prime opportunity to attack. Most of the time the player on the *receiving end* of the short ball will have the best chance of taking the offense.

SUMMARY

As you know, competitive play involves an elastic journey through the three modes: defensive, offensive, and neutral—and although experience is certainly an aid, the tried and true measures outlined above will certainly help level the playing field.

So don't let your opponent's experience intimidate you. Sure, it's an aid—but now you've got countermeasures, and you're ready to make the same kind of high quality choices on your end.

THE "TURNABOUT" TRICK

Q: USUALLY MY OPPONENT IS THE ONE WHO'S CONTROLLING PLAY. HOW CAN I TURN THE TABLES ON THEM?

A: The best way to do that is to be more proactive. A proactive player seeks to impose their will on both the ball and their opponent—whereas a *reactive* player is forced to respond as best they can.

Because tennis is full of emergencies that trigger your basic fight or flight instincts, it can require a real act of will to stay proactive in the face of adversity. But for maximum effectiveness, you need to be both mentally and physically proactive.

- When you're *physically proactive,* you're nice and early with your racket preparation. Your footwork and court positioning are good, and you execute shots with conviction. In moments of uncertainty you instinctively move forward—because you see it as an opportunity to physically impose your will on your opponent.

- When you're *mentally proactive,* you're alert and aggressive in your decision-making processes. You make quick, clear judgments based on all the available information, and you're confident in estimating what needs to be done next.

Any time your opponent does a better job in those areas than you do, they'll probably continue to control play. So to turn things around, ask yourself the following question between every game:

- *"Am I being as proactive as I can reasonably be?"*

The word reasonably is significant here: It factors in variables such as fitness level, skill level, and athletic ability, as well as various other pertinent considerations. The angle of the sun, for instance, can dramatically affect your serve, high volleys and overheads—and make it a lot more difficult to be successful at net from the afflicted end of the court.

- So first consider the variables. Then, if you conclude that you're not being as proactive as you can reasonably be, boldly torque it up a notch.

Whether you're a baseliner, all-courter or serve-volleyer, the ultimate goal is the same: You want to be the one imposing your will on your opponent—and proactive play is the very best way to do that. So show them they're not the boss of you. After all, turnabout is fair play!

THE "ZAP THE BOOGEYMAN" TRICK

Q: IT'S SOOO HARD TO REMEMBER ALL THE THINGS I'M SUPPOSED TO DO! POOR PITIFUL ME! WHAT SHALL I DO—WHAT *SHALL* I DO!

A: Stop whining—that's a bunch of hooey! Whoever started that stuff deserves fifty lashes with a wet noodle.

At first glance, the "Too Many Things To Remember" boogeyman might seem pretty scary. After all, he's a notorious member of the Fear & Doubt gang, and reports from around the world all say the same thing: "He's out to get you!" Luckily, it's pretty easy to outfox him.

- The best way to zap the boogeyman is to say, "I'm only willing to consider two corrections for any given shot." That will freeze him dead in his tracks!

Let's say your forehand is collapsing to the point that you're netting half of them. Now, the boogeyman would just love to see you mind-boggle yourself with fifty pieces of advice; but in truth, all you really need is the *right* advice! Sure, any one of the fifty might help—but definitely not all at once!

The great boxing trainer Teddy Atlas summed it up beautifully. He said:

- "In a closely contested match, it's not enough to just *do things*. You need to do *the right things!*"

So start by selecting a maximum of two corrections. In the case of your errant forehand, you might:

1. Focus on hitting uphill. (See the "Ramp" trick in Groundstroke Magic.)
2. Establish better balance just prior to contact. (See the "Conquistador" trick in Body Magic.)

And if you're too stressed out to deal with two? That's easy: Just focus exclusively on the *single most meaningful correction you can think of that will help you clear the net.*

When you're feeling overwhelmed, narrowing your options can go a long way toward helping you reestablish your poise. After all, the "Too Many Things To Remember" boogeyman is only a paper goblin—and you're more than a match for him. So zap him good by focusing on a maximum of two corrections. That's the very best way to keep that old mind boggler at bay!

THE "ZEN MIND" TRICK

Q: IS THERE A TRICK TO HELP ME TRY HARDER WHEN THINGS ARE GOING POORLY?

A: Maybe "Yes"—maybe "No." Maybe "Yes" *and* "No."

OK . . . Now that you're in Zen mode, you're ready to merge with the void. So melt into this:

- Never try harder. *Just concentrate better!*

As the great Jedi philosopher Yoda once said, "There is no try—there is only do!" That's a great commentary on the concept that "trying" is an inherently losing proposition. The fatal flaw is this:

- "Trying" involves focusing on the effort. But unfortunately, the more you do that, the further you move away from the relaxed state of mind that's most conducive to playing your best tennis.

It's like trying *not to think of a pink elephant* for the next ten seconds: Try that on for size! No wait . . . I mean, don't try. And whatever you do, don't try not to try!

Get it now? There is no try—there is only do!

- So rather than try harder, just relax and commit to a *higher level of concentration!*

Then, run like a deer for each and every shot. You'll be amazed at how far that kind of commitment can take you. Altogether, it's a great recipe for success: Just mix an ounce of Zen with an ounce of desire—and then serve over ice and enjoy!

Part III

The Essential Shots

4
GROUNDSTROKE MAGIC

QUESTIONS	TRICKS	
Open stance or closed stance—which one is better for me?	*Understanding Open And Closed Stance Groundstrokes*	67
What springboard concept can I use to take my rally game to the next level?	*Ramp*	70
How can I develop a more consistent stroke path? Every swing I take feels a little different.	*Finish It*	73
I've heard that I can use my legs to get more power on my groundies. How does that work?	*Power Leg*	82

What "Golden Groundie Rule" should I always keep in mind?	*Early Bird*	87
Everything I hit is going long. How can I keep the ball in the court?	*Big Two, Little Two*	88
Everybody attacks my one-handed backhand. How can I shore up my defense on that side?	*Brush The Crumbs Off The Table*	89
Whenever I'm under pressure I almost always hit the ball in the net. Help me out—I'm sick of being a tennis cliché!	*Fifteen Degrees*	91
During practice, I've heard coaches yell, "Get back to the center!" after every shot. Is the center of the baseline the best place to operate from during a typical rally up the middle?	*Home Base*	92
How can I guarantee that I'll get to more of my opponent's shots?	*Ready, Set, Go!*	94
My backhand isn't bad—but it's definitely not pro-ish. Tune me up?	*String Quartet*	95
I'm under attack and I've lost all confidence in my passing shots. What's the Court of Last Resort for regaining my accuracy?	*Target*	96
I take a really big loop on my groundies. What's "Plan B" if there's not enough time?	*Terminator*	97

UNDERSTANDING OPEN AND CLOSED STANCE GROUNDSTROKES

Q: OPEN STANCE OR CLOSED STANCE—WHICH ONE IS BETTER FOR ME?

A: Both families have their strengths and weaknesses, so the deciding factor often comes down to this:

- "What is it that you want (or need!) to do *after* you hit your shot—and where do you need to go to do that?"

So let's start by looking at some of the advantages and disadvantages of each, bearing in mind that in the open stance family there's a broad variation that ranges from slightly to completely open. Some of the pros and cons listed below are inherent to each category, whereas others are simply related to follow-up actions you might want to take after you make contact with the ball.

OPEN STANCE FOREHAND FAMILY – ADVANTAGES

[Definition: When you stand at-ease facing the net, you're in a *completely* open stance. In this family of stances, your dominant side foot (right foot if you're a righty, left foot if you're a lefty) is placed *closer to the path of the incoming ball* than your other foot.]

- LATERAL MOBILITY – It's easy to recover laterally after you strike the ball. So if you're pulled out wide and want to be able to recover court position, hitting from an open stance makes a lot of sense.
- GOOD POWER – Open stance allows for lots of hip and shoulder rotation into the ball. That facilitates the increased racket head speed that's necessary for a fast, powerful shot.

OPEN STANCE FOREHAND FAMILY – DISADVANTAGE

- FORWARD MOBILITY – In open stance it's more difficult to move *forward* immediately after you strike the ball, because your rapid *lateral core rotation* has to finish before you can advance. And any wraparound racket finish further compounds the problem: As the mass of the racket travels across your body, its momentum naturally pulls you off to that side.

CLOSED STANCE FOREHAND – ADVANTAGES

[Definition: You're in a closed forehand stance when your foot that's *opposite* your dominant (forehand) arm is placed *closer to the path of the incoming ball* than your dominant side foot. See illustration, page 83.]

- FORWARD MOBILITY – It's easy to move forward right behind your strike, because there's less lateral body rotation and/or racket wraparound to hinder you. That's obviously a big advantage when you want to follow an approach shot to the net.
- GOOD POWER – More mass (bodyweight) equals more power—and in closed stance you can easily add bodyweight power by stepping and/or leaning into your shots just prior to contact.
- LOWER RISK/HIGHER CONSISTENCY – Using your body weight to gain additional power is a lot less risky than using an unaccustomedly fast swing speed.

CLOSED STANCE FOREHAND – DISADVANTAGE

- A closed stance can be a huge hindrance to subsequent *lateral* movement, because when you finish your shot, your front leg is momentarily pinned across your body and your hips are locked.
  - So if a ball is to your right and you use a closed stance, it's tough to move quickly to your *left* after contact
  - And if a ball is to your left and you use a closed stance, it's tough to move quickly to your *right* after contact.

Obviously, that's bad news if you're pulled out wide, because you can't even begin to recover back into the court until you first untangle your legs and hips.

Because of that significant liability, the vast majority of forehands in modern baseline rallies are hit in open stance to facilitate quick lateral recovery. Nevertheless, closed stance is always a superb option when you want to add body-weight oomph to a groundstroke or move forward behind an approach shot. In those instances, old-school still rules!

BACKHAND-SPECIFIC ISSUES

- For one-handers, the biomechanics are such that closed stance is always a better backhand option—*if you have time to set up!*

That's because a closed stance backhand allows you to uncoil your core forward into the ball and then out toward your target. In open stance, the uncoiling is much more across the path of the ball, with less extension toward your target—so your timing has to be extremely precise to maintain linear control.

But nothing is an absolute deal-breaker! So never say never: *It's possible to make any shot from any stance*—just as long as you have the requisite athletic ability and talent.

Two-handers, in contrast, have more biomechanical leeway—and although closed stance ruled for decades, an exciting new trend emerged in the women's game in the 1990s. Many WTA pros began using open stance *rally backhands* that virtually mirrored their open stance forehands. It's a dazzling evolution in the game, and the women definitely led the way at the world-class level.

SUMMARY

Because tennis is an open-skill sport (*one in which your opponent is constantly introducing variables*), it's a given that you can't always choose your stance. If a ball is extremely short or wide, you might have to hit closed-stance on the run one second and fend off a jammer from open-stance the next.

- In those situations it's vital to keep your entire focus on making your shot! So trust your innate ability to adjust instinctively—and never worry about your feet.

And when you *are* fortunate enough to enjoy the luxury of choosing a stance, don't forget to factor in the action you intend to take *after* you strike the ball! That's always a critical consideration—and now that you understand the strengths and weaknesses of the different stances, you're well equipped to choose wisely!

THE "RAMP" TRICK

Q: WHAT SPRINGBOARD CONCEPT CAN I USE TO TAKE MY RALLY GAME TO THE NEXT LEVEL?

A: "Over the net, into the court"—that's the bare bones of tennis! The "Big Two, Little Two" and "Finish It" tricks in this chapter will take care of the into the court part—but there's no joy until you take care of the over the net part!

RAMPONICS 101 – Know It!

Visualize yourself in a baseline rally: The ball has bounced in front of you and it's sitting right at your favorite height. Now freeze that image in your mind, and then draw a line straight from the ball toward the net, parallel to the ground.

The net

Zero degrees elevation – No ramp at all

That's what no ramp at all looks like—and occasionally, that will be a perfect choice. But there's one huge caveat:

- It only works if the ball is higher than the net at the moment of contact!

In all other circumstances, the Ramp Rule rules!

THE RAMP RULE

If the ball is lower than the height of the net, you must hit it somewhere on the bottom half and drive it up a ramp.

For more on that—and to fully appreciate how the two tricks complement each other perfectly—I strongly recommend that you refer back to the "Four Quarters" in Key Concepts.

Got it? Great! Now, it's on to Ramponics 102!

RAMPONICS 102 – See It!

There are three basic ramps you can use during a rally: Minimum Ramp, Median Ramp and Maximum Ramp. Below is an illustration of each:

MINIMUM RAMP

Consider using at least 20 degrees of elevation

MEDIAN RAMP

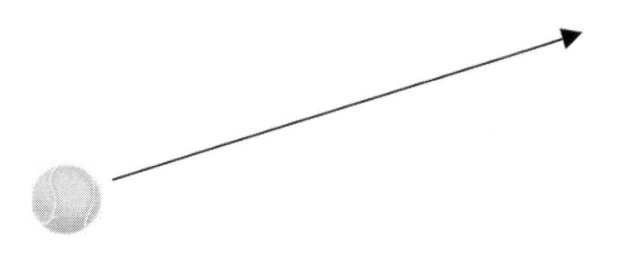

Consider using at least 35 degrees of elevation

MAXIMUM RAMP

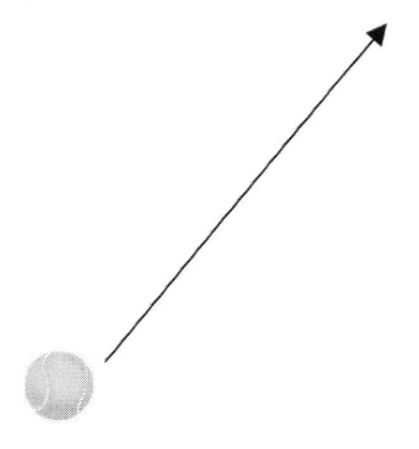

Consider using 50 degrees of elevation—or more!

RAMPONICS 103 – Use It!

The minimum ramp is exactly that—it's the minimum uphill ramp you can use and still expect to clear the net. In a Newtonian universe, gravity rules—so the further you are from the net, the steeper or harder you have to hit to counter its effect.

This ramp is useful when you want to keep the ball low, such as when your opponent has strong volley position, or is in the process of moving in. But remember, "The tape always rises when you're under pressure"—so factor that in if you decide to play skim the net.

MEDIAN RAMP

This ramp is a keystone of a dominant groundstroke game. The additional incline provides plenty of safety in terms of net clearance, and also adds length to your shots. So start with about 35 degrees and experiment from there.

What you're looking for is the uphill angle that consistently sends a well-struck, medium paced groundie deep into your opponent's court. That's your personal median ramp.

MAXIMUM RAMP

Though oft maligned by hard-court players, this one has a lot going for it: It's an essential tool you can use to great advantage on any surface.

The benefits include:

- Safety – It's obviously the safest ramp when your opponent is at the baseline. Short of a complete meltdown, you definitely won't miss this shot in the net!

- Time Management – It's a terrific tactical choice when you get pulled out wide and need extra time to get back. If your opponent chooses not to come in, then by all means use maximum ramp to give yourself time to recover your court position.

- Denial – It's a great way to neutralize a one-hander who has a dangerous topspin backhand, or any player who dislikes high balls. The steep trajectory—especially when coupled with topspin—makes for an explosive combination when you want your shot to kick up above your opponent's power zone.

The only real drawback to maximum ramp is that your shot stays in the air longer—both before and after the bounce. That gives your opponent some additional time to get to it, and also gives them the option of moving forward for a nice, high volley. But all in all, the terrific benefits certainly make Maximum Ramp an option that's well worth exploring.

SUMMARY

There you have it: Know It, See It, and Use It! Those three pillars of the "Ramp" trick are all the support you need to meet any rally challenge. Remember, "Effectiveness is the measure of truth"—and killer effectiveness from the baseline is what this trick is all about. So rev up and ramp up: It's the best way to take your rally game straight to the next level!

THE "FINISH IT" TRICK – Part 1: Introduction

Q: HOW CAN I DEVELOP A MORE CONSISTENT STROKE PATH? EVERY SWING I TAKE FEELS A LITTLE DIFFERENT.

A: Establish a pre-defined finishing point for your hitting hand and racket—and then use that finish whenever your court situation and degree of difficulty allow.

THE "WHY" OF IT

Finishing your shot in a specific location is a great way to embed the new muscle memory you need for consistent strokes. So when you first start working on this, don't worry too much about where your shots are landing. Instead, stay focused on your finish.

- It doesn't matter whether you hit a good shot, a bad shot, or even completely miss the ball. Just do the reps, and focus on achieving that *ideal finish after contact,* each and every time.

If you're disciplined and stay with it, you'll see dramatic improvement in the consistency of your stroke path—and soon, anything other than that finish will feel downright awkward and unnatural.

THE "WHERE" OF IT

So *where* exactly is that ideal finish? Well, that depends:

- *Your preferred grip is a vital part of the equation.* Due to natural biomechanics, most players who use a particular grip tend to finish their strokes in the same general area.

So in Part Two we'll take a look at some tried and true finishes for the four groundstrokes—topspin and underspin forehand, and topspin and underspin backhand—and how the various grips factor in.

FINISH IT – Part 2: Forehands

TOPSPIN FOREHAND FINISH IT

There are four grips you can use to hit a topspin forehand.

1. Semi-western grip
2. Eastern grip
3. Full Western grip
4. Continental grip

The following diagram indicates where a right-hander should center the *palm-side base knuckle* of their index finger for each grip. (For more on grips, see Chapter 2.)

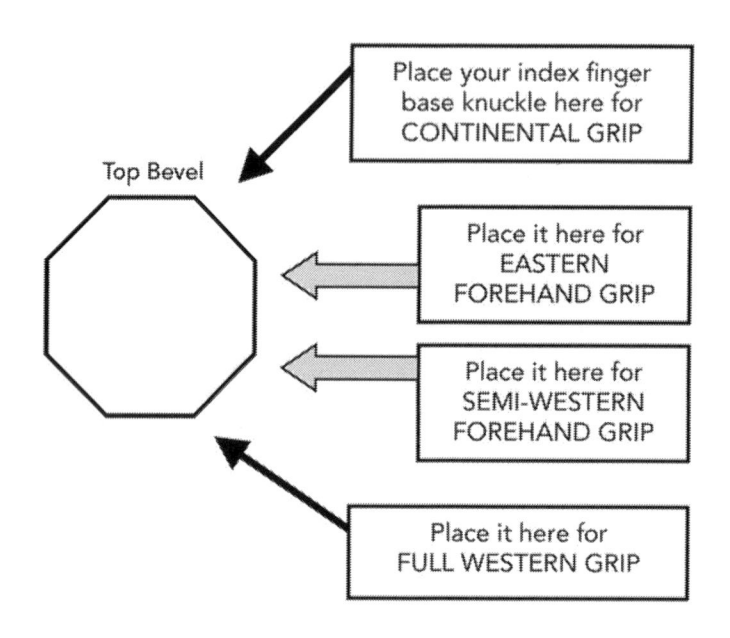

Now, let's start with Semi-western, which is the forehand rally grip used by the majority of high-level players in this first decade of the 21st century.

1. **IN SEMI-WESTERN GRIP, YOUR IDEAL FINISH IS OFTEN OVER YOUR NON-DOMINANT SHOULDER.**

To find it, first make a fist with your dominant hand. Then place that thumbnail on top of your non-dominant shoulder, and raise your pinky knuckle a little until you can easily kiss the back of that hand.

That pinky up, thumb down rotation of your hand and forearm is called pronation. It's the ideal finishing *posture* for that hand and arm, because it safely releases the stress imposed by the stroke.

Now grab your racket and find an unobstructed area where you're free to swing through your full forehand motion. Finish your stroke over your opposite shoulder as described above, and then—*just as a test*—tilt your head slightly in that direction. If your hand is in the right area and correctly pronated, you'll be able to easily touch your pinky knuckle with your ear. Obviously, you will *not* tilt your head that way during play. (See photo)

HERE'S A TYPICAL
SEMI-WESTERN
TOPSPIN
FOREHAND FINISH

---

2. **IN EASTERN FOREHAND GRIP, YOUR IDEAL FINISH CAN BE MORE OUT IN FRONT IN THE DIRECTION OF YOUR TARGET.**

If you have a fast swing it's fine to let the racket head travel toward your non-dominant side after contact. Just be sure to pronate enough to relieve any stress on your wrist and arm.

HERE'S A TYPICAL EASTERN TOPSPIN FOREHAND FINISH

3. IN FULL WESTERN GRIP, YOUR IDEAL FINISH WILL PROBABLY BE LOWER THAN THE OVER THE SHOULDER FINISH OF THE SEMI-WESTERN PLAYER.

This is a fast, wristy stroke: The initial forward racket motion is upward—but then moves rapidly across the body in a windshield wiper-like arc. The end result is that the hitting hand often finishes below shoulder height, approximately level with the non-dominant armpit or rib cage. When you use your wrist like that you absolutely *must* pronate after contact to reduce the risk of injury.

HERE'S A TYPICAL FULL WESTERN TOPSPIN FOREHAND FINISH

4. IN CONTINENTAL GRIP, A LOW-TO-HIGH SWING IS PRIORITY NUMBER ONE FOR TOPSPIN!

Although Continental is a wonderfully versatile grip, the more open racket face doesn't generate any *inherent topspin:* You have to consciously create it with a pronounced low-to-high swing. The wrinkle is, the higher the ball bounces the tougher it is to do that, so don't count on dominating most topspin baseline rallies with this grip.

Often, your best topspin play will be an opportunistic attack in which you sling the ball forward and charge the net as fast as you can. Once you're up there, your Continental grip is ideally suited for volleys and overheads. So be confident and aggressive; McEnroe, Edberg and Navratilova did it, and so can you!

UNDERSPIN FOREHAND FINISH IT

Many players like to use Continental grip for underspin shots—but whatever grip you use, you need to apply an open, beveled racket face at contact. Then, continue moving your racket hand out toward the target—with your palm beveled up toward the sky, and your knuckles down toward the court. Do keep a little bend in your elbow prior to contact, and finish with good forward extension.

HERE'S A TYPICAL CONTINENTAL UNDERSPIN FOREHAND FINISH

A word of caution about hacking and hewing: In general, you'll have a better chance of making an accurate shot if you keep your wrist nice and firm. Yes, wrist action can do wonders—but there's a small margin for error in terms of timing.

Now, that's certainly not to say, "No hacking allowed!" If you enjoy that style and it works for you, by all means go for it! Who's to say you're not a bona fide French Chef, tricky enough to carve your opponent to pieces. So if that's you—and you know who you are—then slice and dice to your heart's content. Get out there and drive your opponents ca-raazy—and bon appétit!

FINISH IT – Part 3: Backhands and Summary

Once again, a consistent, pre-defined finish is the key.

TOPSPIN BACKHAND FINISH IT – One-Handers

Regardless of grip, one-handers benefit greatly from full extension after contact, because the longer their strings stay on track toward the target, the more accurate and penetrating the shot will be. So drive your racket head out in the direction you want the ball to travel, and finish up high for good topspin.

HERE'S A TYPICAL
ONE-HANDED
TOPSPIN
BACKHAND FINISH

TOPSPIN BACKHAND FINISH IT – Two-Handers

No shot in modern tennis is struck with greater uniformity than the two-handed topspin backhand: Agassi, Roddick, and the William sisters are just a few outstanding models.

And although there's a fair amount of variation in the top players' grips, most of them finish that shot in almost exactly the same place.

- The vast majority of the time they finish over the opposite shoulder—with the knuckles of their helping hand fully pronated and very close to their ear.

That means the top edge and bottom edge of the racket wind up reversed—in that the edge that *was on top* at contact finishes flipped down toward their opposite shoulder.

The over the shoulder finish is quintessential tried and true, and it's a great model—but never hesitate to improvise if you're off balance. In an emergency situation, anything goes—and an ugly shot that lands in the court is *always* better than a gorgeous, technically perfect shot that misses!

HERE'S A TYPICAL
TWO-HANDED
TOPSPIN
BACKHAND FINISH

UNDERSPIN BACKHAND FINISH IT – One-Handers

Most players choose to use Continental grip for underspin backhands. But regardless of grip, you need to apply an open, beveled racket face at contact.

- A high-to-low stroke with a *low finish* works well for both drop shots and approach shots—and if you want extra loft or length on a particular shot, you can finish out high-and-away.

If you're in a mood to slice-and-dice, you might elect to carve across the ball for a tricky sidespin shot. But remember—that's a true skill shot, because there's so little time during which your strings are actually *guiding the ball forward*. In general, the longer you guide the ball forward and keep your strings moving out toward your target, the better your accuracy and/or penetration will be.

HERE'S A TYPICAL ONE-HANDED UNDERSPIN BACKHAND FINISH

UNDERSPIN BACKHAND FINISH IT – Two-Handers

The key points that apply to one-handers apply to you as well. Set an open, beveled racket face prior to contact, and then finish by moving your strings out toward your target as far as you can.

HERE'S A TYPICAL TWO-HANDED UNDERSPIN BACKHAND FINISH

The bad news is, as a two hander, that won't be very far at all—because holding the racket with both hands severely limits your ability to extend after contact.

- That's why many two-handers choose to release their helping hand when they hit underspin, and play it just like a one-hander. They realize that what they lose in support, they gain in extension—which usually translates into increased accuracy and/or penetration.

If you elect to do that, just follow the one-hander's underspin guidelines. A high-to-low stroke with a *low finish* works well for both drop shots and approach shots—and if you want extra loft or length on a particular shot, you can finish out high-and-away.

SUMMARY

Although the various grip and finish combinations we've looked at for forehand and backhand are tried and true, they're certainly not mandatory. So use them as a starting point on your individual journey of self-discovery, and have fun exploring the possibilities. Then, when you find a pre-defined finish that works well for you, just stick with it to reap the benefits that spring from consistent technique.

- Remember, the major benefit of a set finish is that it builds the muscle memory that's essential for consistent, quality strokes. The more you repeat a finish, the more you'll embed it in your muscle memory, and that's what this trick is all about.

Fortified with that embedded muscle memory, you'll be much better equipped to go for your shots when you're tired, nervous or confused—rather than trying to push or steer the ball around the court.

So "Finish It" as often as you can, whenever your court situation and degree of difficulty allow. Then, warn your opponent to watch out for guided missiles, and let the punishment begin!

THE "POWER LEG" TRICK

Q: I'VE HEARD THAT I CAN USE MY LEGS TO GET MORE POWER ON MY GROUNDIES. HOW DOES THAT WORK?

A: You're right—you can get lots of extra power from your legs. The principles are the same for forehand and backhand—but because the precise how-to varies depending on your stance, we'll look at each side separately.

THE FOREHAND POWER LEG – OPEN STANCE

- In open stance, the leg *under your hitting arm* is your power leg.

HERE'S A TYPICAL OPEN STANCE FOREHAND

Hip and shoulder rotation are key elements of an open stance shot, so it's important to get your power foot closer to the back fence than your front foot. That way you can load your weight onto that back leg, and then rotate your hip and shoulder forward into the ball for power.

THE FOREHAND POWER LEG – CLOSED STANCE

- In closed stance, *your back leg is your power leg.* That's the leg you push forward with to transfer body weight into your shot.

**HERE'S A TYPICAL
CLOSED STANCE
FOREHAND**

Your front foot can be a great anchor—providing stability and balance that will greatly contribute to your effectiveness—but it's *not* your power leg. It's your stability leg! Once you're all set up for your shot in closed stance, that's the function of your front leg. So for maximum stability, bend your knees and drop your hips so your thigh muscles support your weight in a stable hitting position prior to your final action. Then, you can either press up *or* leap up into the ball for explosive power!

THE ONE-HANDED BACKHAND POWER LEG – OVERVIEW

- If you use a one-handed backhand, you'll generally be far more effective hitting from a closed stance.

THE ONE-HANDED BACKHAND POWER LEG – CLOSED STANCE

- In closed stance, your back leg is your power leg. That's the leg you push forward with to transfer body weight into your shots.

Yes, your front foot can be a great anchor—providing vital stability and balance—but it's *not* your power leg. It's your stability leg! Once you're all set up for your shot in closed stance, that's the function of your front leg. So load your weight onto your lead foot, and then bend your front knee so you can drop your hips nice and low. That will allow your thigh and gluteus muscles to support your body in an extremely stable hitting position.

HERE'S A TYPICAL
CLOSED STANCE
ONE-HANDED BACKHAND

THE ONE-HANDED BACKHAND POWER LEG – OPEN STANCE

This shot is seldom seen—and for good reason! It's basically an emergency shot that most players only hit when they absolutely have to. Biomechanically, it's the weakest way to hit a one-handed backhand, and neither leg really offers much help as a power leg. Obviously, there will be times when you have to use it—but don't count on your legs for much help. Any success you achieve will be derived wholly from your body rotation, timing and talent.

THE TWO-HANDED BACKHAND POWER LEG – OVERVIEW

- You guys have options! You can hit from the traditional 20th century closed stance, or you can use the open stance option that's become increasingly popular in the early 21st Century.

THE TWO-HANDED BACKHAND POWER LEG – CLOSED STANCE

A closed stance two-handed backhand offers all the same waist-down advantages as a closed stance one-handed backhand.

- In closed stance, your back leg is your power leg. That's the leg you push forward with to transfer body weight into your shots.

HERE'S A TYPICAL CLOSED STANCE TWO-HANDED BACKHAND

Yes, your front foot can be a great anchor—providing vital stability and balance—but it's *not* your power leg. It's your stability leg! Once you're all set up for your shot in closed stance, that's the function of your front leg. So load your weight onto your lead foot, and then bend your front knee so you can drop your hips nice and low. That will allow your thigh and gluteus muscles to support your body in an extremely stable hitting position.

THE TWO-HANDED BACKHAND POWER LEG – OPEN STANCE

An open stance two-handed backhand offers all the same waist-down advantages as an open stance forehand.

- For right-handers, your *open stance backhand* power leg will be your left leg—the leg closest to the *path* of the ball when you're facing the net—and vice-versa for lefties.

HERE'S A TYPICAL
OPEN STANCE
TWO-HANDED BACKHAND

Your two-handed set-up can be pretty much a mirror image of your open stance forehand set-up. Core rotation is a key element of an open stance shot, so in both instances you want to set up with your power foot closer to the back fence than your front foot. That will enable you to maximize your hip and shoulder rotation into the ball.

SUMMARY

Now that you understand how to utilize your legs in shot making, you'll be able to accomplish a lot more without swinging harder. Power well applied is without a doubt an important part of a well-rounded game. So whenever possible, use your power and anchor legs correctly to generate the extra zip that can turn a good shot into a great one!

THE "EARLY BIRD" TRICK

Q: WHAT "GOLDEN GROUNDIE RULE" SHOULD I ALWAYS KEEP IN MIND?

A: "The early bird (often) gets the point!" The early bird is the player who never lags in their preparation.

Because tennis is often a rapid-fire game of action and reaction, early preparation is a key fundamental.

- The sooner you start, the more relaxed and thoughtful you can be regarding whatever needs to be done next.

But if you're late getting ready, things can get dicey—and you might be forced to rely on either:

- Brute strength (Fine if you can pull it off.) Or . . .
- Improvisational skill (Fine if you can pull it off!)

Either one can save you in a pinch, but neither is a suitable replacement for good old early preparation.

So whether you loop or take your racket straight back on your groundies, get going with it as soon as you can. Early birds earn a small but mighty advantage. They always have just a little bit more time to apply their favorite Tennis Magic tricks, and that makes for a simple, happy equation: The more time you have, the more magic you can work!

THE "BIG TWO, LITTLE TWO" TRICK

Q: EVERYTHING I HIT IS GOING LONG. HOW CAN I KEEP THE BALL IN THE COURT?

A: Start by using the "Big Two":

1. *Ask* the ball to come down by swinging from low to high for topspin.

2. *Finish* your shot completely whenever circumstances allow.

(Regarding *Ask*, See "The Ball Is My Friend" in Key Concepts. Regarding *Finish*, see the "Finish It" trick in this chapter.)

The physics of topspin is simple: The more racket speed you use while hitting from low-to-high, the faster the ball will rotate forward. (More revolutions per minute generate more friction between the ball and the air—and that friction is what pushes the ball down toward the court.)

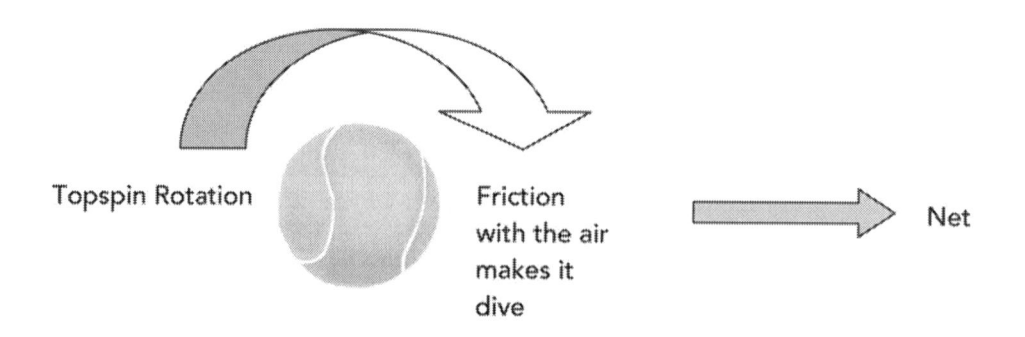

OK . . . So far, so good! But what if you're already applying nice topspin and your shots are still going long?

In that case, do some fine-tuning with the "Little Two":

1. Make sure you're not opening up your racket face just prior to contact. (Simply put, that means don't angle your strings up toward the sky too much.) If your racket face is too open at contact, not even a perfect finish will help: Just say, "Buh-bye"—because that ball may *never* come down!)

2. Make sure you're using *your* right grip. ("Your" right grip means the grip you truly intend to use for the shot you want to hit.)

That should take care of the loose ends—but keep in mind that those are supplemental corrections. The most important thing to do when you want to control the length of your shots is to *focus on a low-to-high swing combined with a good finish.* That's a sure-fire way to get back on track quicker than you can say "Big Two, Little Two!"

THE "BRUSH THE CRUMBS OFF THE TABLE" TRICK – Part 1

Q: EVERYBODY ATTACKS MY ONE-HANDED BACKHAND. HOW CAN I SHORE UP MY DEFENSE ON THAT SIDE?

A: Brush some crumbs off the table to refine your Continental grip underspin shot!

This trick will help you handle almost any backhand emergency, and provides a solid foundation for converting potentially tricky midcourt challenges into offensive opportunities.

First, let's do a run-through so you can feel it physically. You'll need two props—a chair, and any straight edged desk or dining table.

> Step 1: Pull up your chair close to the front edge of a desk or table—then turn sideways so that your hitting arm is right next to it. Now lay your elbow, forearm and palm flat down on the table, right along that front edge.
>
> Step 2: Next, point your nose across the table and lean in that direction until your chin is over your forearm. That's what it feels like from the waist up to lean your body weight into a backhand for maximum penetration on your shot.
>
> Step 3: Finally, brush your hand, forearm and elbow smoothly away from you to brush some imaginary crumbs straight across the table.

Keep the whole unit from elbow to pinky knuckle in a nice straight line, and let your chin follow your arm as you brush out about twelve to fifteen inches toward the far side. Make sure you *brush straight across the table,* without angling off toward the side.

Well done—you're almost there! In Part 2 we'll add some bevel to that shot so it clears the net *and* stays low after it bounces.

BRUSH THE CRUMBS OFF THE TABLE – Part 2

Once again, start by sitting sideways to the table with your forearm resting parallel to the near edge. Then, lift your thumb and rotate your forearm forward a little until your thumb and index finger are about two inches above the surface.

As you look at the back of your hand you'll see a bevel of about 45 degrees. That's a great visual cue: In Continental grip, "What you see is what you get"—so the angle of your strings is always identical to the angle of the back of your hand!

Now that you've set your bevel, you're ready to brush crumbs—and it's Part One "Déjà vu all over again" . . .

- First, remain sideways and lean toward the far side of the table. That's how you'll transfer body weight into your shot for maximum penetration.

- Next, brush crumbs across the table—keeping your hand and forearm in that 45 degree beveled position. Make sure that the near edge of your hand remains slightly above the table, while the far edge of your hand stays *on* the table.

- As you brush, keep the whole unit from elbow to pinky knuckle in a nice straight line. Sweep the crumbs *straight across the table*—not off to the side—and keep brushing out twelve to fifteen inches as you lean in that direction.

Voila—you're there! That's what it feels like to hit a great underspin backhand. As long as you're in continental grip, sweeping your hand out toward your target will feel wonderfully smooth and natural. Whether it's a volley or a groundstroke, a high ball or a low one, you're ready for anything!

As you can see, this trick is a great combination package. Your backhand defense will be stronger from the baseline, and you'll be a lot tougher in midcourt as well. Now you can knife that short ball and move right in behind it. Your shot will have automatic underspin to help keep it low after it bounces, and the more you lean into it, the more penetrating it will be.

So start today. Use Continental grip underspin to brush away your backhand blues just as easily as you brushed those crumbs off the table!

THE "FIFTEEN DEGREES" TRICK

Q: WHENEVER I'M UNDER PRESSURE I ALMOST ALWAYS HIT THE BALL IN THE NET. HELP ME OUT—I'M SICK OF BEING A TENNIS CLICHÉ!

A: Avoid that cliché by using a steeper ramp! (For an in-depth explanation of ramps, see the "Ramp" trick in Groundstroke Magic.)

Start by visualizing your favorite ramp—the one you tend to use most often during a rally for consistent net clearance and good depth of shot.

Your Favorite Rally Ramp

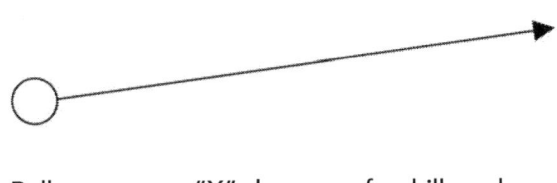

The Ball   "X" degrees of uphill angle

Now, we know that ramp works fine until you're under pressure, so this is an easy fix. Just add an additional 15 degrees to create your emergency Pressure Ramp!

Your Pressure Ramp

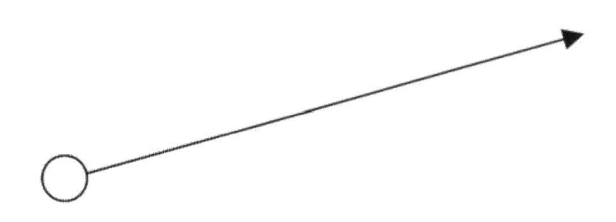

The Ball   "X" degrees *plus an additional 15 degrees* of uphill angle

Your Pressure Ramp can be a real lifesaver in any of the following circumstances:

- Anytime you're caught in a cycle of repeatedly netting your passing shots.
- Anytime you're pulled out so wide on court that you're out of your comfort zone.
- Anytime your opponent hits a knifing underspin shot. That ball will usually stay

very low after it bounces—and if you decide to answer with topspin from way down there, you'll often need that extra 15 degrees of uphill angle just to clear the net!

And last, but certainly not least, there's plain old "Feeling the heat!"—for whatever reason at all. But regardless of the source of the pressure, no worries. Just remember to switch to your elevated ramp, and then relax and go for it fearlessly. That fifteen degrees is pure gold, and it's the key to beating the "Into the net again!" cliché. As soon as you start adding that fifteen degrees, it's onward and *upward* for you!

THE "HOME BASE" TRICK

Q: DURING PRACTICE, I'VE HEARD COACHES YELL, "GET BACK TO THE CENTER!" AFTER EVERY SHOT. IS THE CENTER OF THE BASELINE THE BEST PLACE TO OPERATE FROM DURING A TYPICAL RALLY UP THE MIDDLE?

A: Most of the time, it's not! When your opponent is striking from *their* center baseline area, your ideal home base is more toward the sideline on your *weaker* side.

There are two great reasons to hedge that way a little bit, rather than set up in the true "bisect their available angle" location. First, let's look at how it works when your opponent is striking from more or less the center section of the court:

1. IF YOU HAVE A *WEAKER DEFENSIVE SIDE,* SHADE HOME BASE IN THAT DIRECTION!

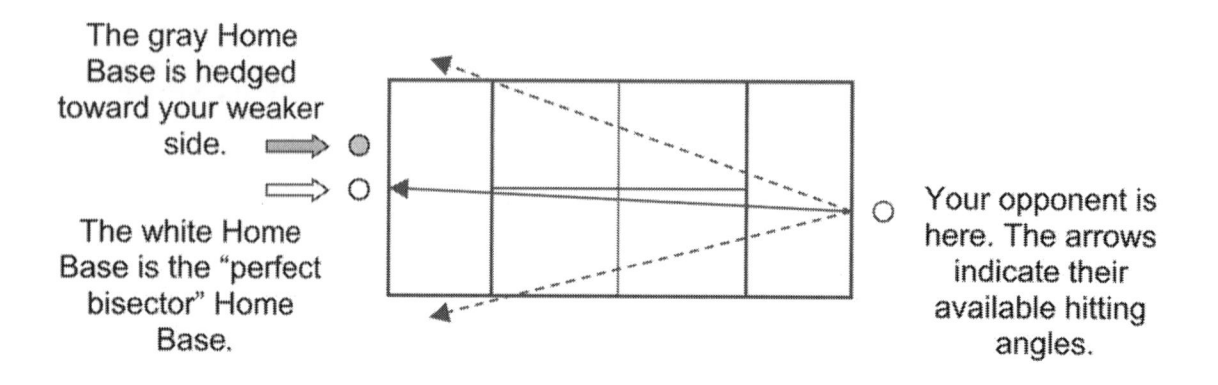

The gray Home Base is hedged toward your weaker side.

The white Home Base is the "perfect bisector" Home Base.

Your opponent is here. The arrows indicate their available hitting angles.

THE REASON – Obviously, you'll be able to hit on balance a lot more often if you don't have to run so far to defend your weaker side.

So go ahead and over-shift as much as you like in that direction—*just as long as you can still get to most balls on your stronger side in time to hit a good shot!* That's the determining factor in how far you can safely shift your home base.

2. IF YOUR DEFENSE IS EQUALLY SOLID OFF BOTH WINGS, THEN SHADE HOME BASE *TOWARD YOUR LESS EXPLOSIVE OFFENSIVE SIDE*.

THE REASON – That way you'll be able to run around slow balls that come straight at you, and then attack them with your best offensive weapon.

SHIFTING HOME BASE LATERALLY DURING PLAY

Obviously, when your opponent's shot is going to come from an area to the left or right of the center section, you do need to shift your position laterally toward the area they might realistically attack. But the same considerations discussed above still apply—so you can hedge your bet in the same way, rather than focusing on setting up on the perfect defensive bisector.

SHIFTING HOME BASE FORWARD AND BACKWARD

How far behind (or in front!) of the baseline you choose to play is the other consideration, and that's really a matter of personal preference:

- As long as you can still handle your opponent's pace and average depth of shot, you can move home base forward to a more offensive location. But that decision ultimately depends on your style, your personality, your reflexes, the court surface, and the velocity and/or depth of your opponent's shots.

Now that you understand the key considerations in establishing a personal home base, you'll be able to play a much more relaxed and balanced game. And not only will you be a tough nut to crack defensively—you'll also be poised to unleash your best offensive fireworks at every opportunity. Ah, yes . . . Home, Sweet Home!

THE "READY, SET, GO!" TRICK

Q: HOW CAN I GUARANTEE THAT I'LL GET TO MORE OF MY OPPONENT'S SHOTS?

A: If you're having trouble getting to shots that aren't all that far away from you, it might be because you have your weight loaded on the wrong leg just as your opponent makes contact with the ball.

- The best way to correct that is to take a check step every time they're about to swing.

Lots of intermediate players take check steps on their way to the net, but they don't always use them at the baseline the way most advanced players do.

- If you watch pros *after* they strike the ball, you'll see that they take check steps repeatedly throughout the course of a point. That's because they understand that taking well-timed check steps during a baseline rally can make all the difference in whether or not they get to the next shot.

If you're at all fuzzy about how check steps work, just review the "My Checkered Path" trick in Key Concepts. Once you've got it mesmerized, you're all ready for "Ready, Set, Go!"

1. READY – Time your check step so that you land just before your opponent's strings strike the ball.

2. SET – Land with your weight slightly forward, and evenly distributed on the balls of your feet. From that stance you can easily start to move in the right direction for whatever needs to be done next.

3. GO! – Get going!

Obviously, in defensive emergencies it's fine to skip ready/set and just go: Covering a wide-open court is always your first priority. But in more ambiguous situations when you're uncertain of your opponent's intent, check steps are pure gold.

So use them at every opportunity; they'll set you up for the quick starts that make all the difference in reaching those tough shots. This trick is guaranteed to keep you more on the balls of your feet—and that's a huge help when it comes to getting your feet to more balls!

THE "STRING QUARTET" TRICK

Q: MY BACKHAND ISN'T BAD—BUT IT'S DEFINITELY NOT PRO-ISH. TUNE ME UP?

A: A perfectly struck backhand is truly a thing of beauty, and the sound is music to the ears. And as a great Maestro once said, "There's a little Vivaldi in all of us." So use this trick to create your own beautiful sonata on court!

Here's the score:

> 1st Movement: Go and find the ball as quickly as you can!

> 2nd Movement: As you complete your racket preparation, show the back of your dominant shoulder to the ball. If you have indeed turned your torso sufficiently, your chin will almost touch that shoulder.

> 3rd Movement: If you get there in time, use your power leg for either maximum weight transfer or maximum rotation. (See "The Power Leg" trick in this chapter.)

> 4th Movement: Finish your shot as if you mean it! One handers, use full extension out toward your target unless there's a compelling reason not to do so. Two-handers, finish over your opposite shoulder unless there's a compelling reason not to do so.

That's it. So let the music begin, and use those four movements to play your backhand sonata. If you do, there's an excellent chance you can keep your opponents moaning the blues!

THE "TARGET" TRICK

Q: I'M UNDER ATTACK AND I'VE LOST ALL CONFIDENCE IN MY PASSING SHOTS. WHAT'S THE COURT OF LAST RESORT FOR REGAINING MY ACCURACY?

A: Regain your accuracy by using your pesky opponent as a target!

When you're spraying your passing shots against a relentless net rusher, tennis can be about as much fun as a stubbed toe. But don't despair—even if you've exhausted all your other tricks, there's still one more option.

- The next time they come in to the net, wind up and drive the ball right at them—just as hard as you can!

I mean really go for it—no pussyfooting around! Heck, you're losing all those points anyway, so why not? Granted, it's a low percentage play—but sometimes radical circumstances call for a radical response.

- When you hit right at your opponent, you take away any advantage they might gain by correctly guessing which side to cover. And if you blast away with enough gusto, they just might get gun-shy about coming in so often.

In any event, this much is guaranteed: Every time you target that pesky net-rusher you'll help fine-tune your directional accuracy. And as you regain your striking confidence, it'll become a lot easier to start making some passing shots.

A word to the wise here—and let me phrase it as strongly as I can:

- **TRYING TO HIT THROUGH A GOOD VOLLEYER IS ALMOST ALWAYS A LOSING PROPOSITION!**

Not impossible by any means—just very, very hard to do on a consistent basis.

So think of the "Target" trick as the court of last resort for regaining your accuracy. After all, it never hurts to file one final appeal. And even if the verdict goes against you, at least you'll have the satisfaction of knowing you tried everything!

THE "TERMINATOR" TRICK

Q: I TAKE A REALLY BIG LOOP ON MY GROUNDIES. WHAT'S "PLAN B" IF THERE'S NOT ENOUGH TIME?

A: That's a job for the Terminator!

Just show your strings to the ball with a minimal back swing, and then either rotate into it *or* step into it.

Let's say a ball has gotten in on you sooner than you expected. Maybe your opponent hit it really hard, or maybe you've gotten caught in midcourt. In either case, with limited preparation time, a huge loop is out of the question.

That's when you need to show your strings to the ball as quickly as you can—either by taking your racket straight back or by just laying back your wrist. Then, depending on your stance—which you may or may not have time to adjust—you can either rotate your trunk or step into your shot.

Then, if you use a quick strike aimed at the bottom inside corner of the ball, there's not a lot that can go wrong.

- The Terminator is a topspin shot, so drive up and out through the ball as smartly as you can. (See the "Four Quarters" trick in Key Concepts.) Swing low to high for topspin, and let the finish take care of itself.

Sticklers for detail should be aware that the Terminator does have a flat shot cousin. His name is Terminator II, and he's sort of a loose canon—but occasionally he's just the man for the job. So think Terminator I topspin for safety, and save Terminator II for situations in which the reward warrants the risk.

The true twin to this shot is the Predator in Chapter Six, "Return of Serve Magic." The only difference here is that you're delivering a lethal counter-punch *during the course of a rally* rather than as a service return. So when time is of the essence, think "Terminator." From start to finish it's short, compact and deadly—and it's only fair: They pressured you into it, and now they must pay!

5
SERVICE MAGIC

QUESTIONS	TRICKS	
I'm pretty good about getting my serve *somewhere* in the box—but I could really use some help with my accuracy. What's the trick to putting it right where I want it?	*Palm It*	101
Was there a trick to Pete Sampras' incredible serve—one that I can use too?	*Spear – AKA: King Pete*	103
How can I get more spin on my serves? I just can't seem to do it.	*Grip Trick – Serve*	105
Double faults are killing me! What should I do first?	*First Serve In*	107
OK . . . I've been in a service slump for about two years now! Is there any way I can bust out of it, or am I doomed to life in hell?	*Slump Buster*	108

How do I get my second serve in the box? I'm always afraid I'll double fault!	Archery	109
How can I move in more quickly when I serve-volley? I hardly ever make it in all the way to the service line for my first shot.	Finish Line – AKA: Hip Trick	110
My service motion feels all cramped and weird. How can I smooth it out so I can get more power on my serve?	I Can See Clearly Now	111
My serve is really erratic: Sometimes it's great, but other times it's awful! How can I fix that?	Lock On Target	113
I miss an awful lot of serves in the net. What's the first thing I should do to cure that *fault*?	Nose To The Ball	114
How can I add some speed to my serve? I'm pretty sure I hit one over 50 mph once . . . but my friends say I'm dreaming!	Swish	115
How can I get my service toss under control? It's all over the place!	Don't Let Go	116
How can I still serve effectively when I get all nervous and tight?	Pot Of Gold	117

THE "PALM IT" TRICK

Q: I'M PRETTY GOOD ABOUT GETTING MY SERVE *SOMEWHERE* IN THE BOX—BUT I COULD REALLY USE SOME HELP WITH MY ACCURACY. WHAT'S THE TRICK TO PUTTING IT RIGHT WHERE I WANT IT?

A: Palm it! That's the pro-ish way to get great side-to-side location on your serves.

Although you can serve using any grip, there's a good reason why virtually all advanced players use either Continental grip or a close relative.

Here's the advantage:

- In Continental, the plane of your palm *is an identical match* to the plane of your strings.
    - *So whatever direction your palm is facing when you strike your serve is exactly the direction the ball will travel as it leaves your strings!*

Obviously, that makes it easy to maintain lateral accuracy if you're hitting a fairly flat serve.

- All you have to do is turn an imaginary eye in the center of your palm in the precise direction you want the ball to go, prior to striking it!

You can get a feel for this in thirty seconds. Just place the palm of your serving hand against your ear, and then slowly extend that arm out toward any object in the room (or in your field of vision). Then repeat that motion several times—but each time turn your palm flat out toward a different object in your field of vision.

- That's what it feels like to select your target with your palm. And that's how you "Palm It" for maximum accuracy on your serve.

Now remember: Your palm and strings are a matched set in Continental grip—and the flatter they are to the ball at contact, the longer it will stay on line. Boy, does that make things easy!

- So if you want to serve fairly flat up the center tee, all you have to do is make sure *your palm is looking in that direction as you strike the ball.*
    - And if you want to serve out toward the far corner of the box, just make sure your palm is looking in *that* direction as you strike the ball.

And if you want to serve right at your opponent's belly button?

- Yes, of course! Just show your palm in *that* direction as you strike the ball.

Naturally, if you choose to slice your serve—which is easy to do in Continental grip—the ball will curve after it leaves your strings. But the *initial direction* of the ball will always be exactly where your palm is facing when you strike it. That offers a great permanent reference point for any calculations you need to make.

So if you're wise enough to realize that nothing trumps accuracy, this is the trick you've been looking for. Sure, raw speed is awesome, but it's never enough at a peer level—and no matter how fast you serve, a good athlete will eventually start to return the ones they can reach. That's why accuracy is Queen for keeping your opponent off balance. No degree of athleticism offers protection against great location—and once you start to "Palm It," you'll keep your opponents guessing, and yourself in control!

THE "SPEAR" TRICK – AKA: KING PETE

Q: WAS THERE A TRICK TO PETE SAMPRAS' INCREDIBLE SERVE—ONE THAT I CAN USE TOO?

A: You bet. Think "Spear It"—because it's all about the finish!

Pete Sampras had the most effective, dominant serve in the history of the men's game, and could inflict tremendous damage with his first serve. But it was his second serve that really elevated him to the Top of the Pops: It was only slightly less lethal than his first serve, and double faults were as rare as hens' teeth.

Pete's secret really isn't a secret at all: It's hidden in plain sight in countless photos and film clips. It was all about where the tip of his racket pointed at the *finish* of his service motion.

- It pointed straight down toward the court, with the butt cap straight up toward the sky—just as if the racket was a spear he was plunging into the ground.

That tip down finish is what made the ball dive so sharply into the service box at the last second. And while Sampras was neither the first nor the only player to use that trick, he *was* the first to apply it so uncompromisingly on both first *and second serves.*

Remember, *the beauty of a trick* is that it's virtually bulletproof: All you have to do is commit to it. Pete's commitment to the Spear was total, and it packed a double whammy:

- It allowed him to really go for the lines on his first serve—because he knew that even if he missed, he could still pound his second serve!
  - All he had to do was pick a *slightly* safer target, and then aim a little higher over the net to compensate for the tremendous Spear dive.

Pete was supremely confident that the trick would work for him, and boy, did it ever! And the best news is it'll work wonders for you as well—and it's so easy you'll have it mesmerized in no time.

In order to get the maximum benefit, you need to use Continental or slight backhand grip when you serve. No fudging or whining about that: Just accept the challenge and enter the world of real serving!

Here's the sequence:

- Toss a ball and then start your upward swing as if you're going to hatchet it with the bottom (pinky finger) edge of your racket.

- As you swing up, pronate—which means start rotating your palm out toward the ball. Remember, in Continental grip, wherever your palm is pointing at contact is where your strings are pointing at contact—and that's the line along which a flat serve will travel when you strike it.

- Finally, continue pronating *after* contact until you can see the back of your hand—and then, Spear It!
  - "Spear It" means drive the tip of your racket straight down toward the ground like a spear—with the butt-cap pointing straight up to the sky.

That final action is the clincher: It'll make the ball dive like nobody's business. It's pure magic, and if you believe it and use it like "King Pete" did, this trick should have everyone bowing down to your new serve. But hey, you deserve it—so let the coronation begin!

THE "GRIP" TRICK – SERVE

Q: HOW CAN I GET MORE SPIN ON MY SERVES? I JUST CAN'T SEEM TO DO IT.

A: It's a grip trick—and there's no way to *avoid hitting a spin serve* when you use it!

All it takes is a tiny grip change to add both spin and weight to your serve. Start by holding the racket in Continental grip: Then use your non-dominant hand to rotate your racket ever so slightly toward backhand grip (that's clockwise if you're a right-handed server, counterclockwise if you're a lefty). Voila! That small grip change *is* the magic.

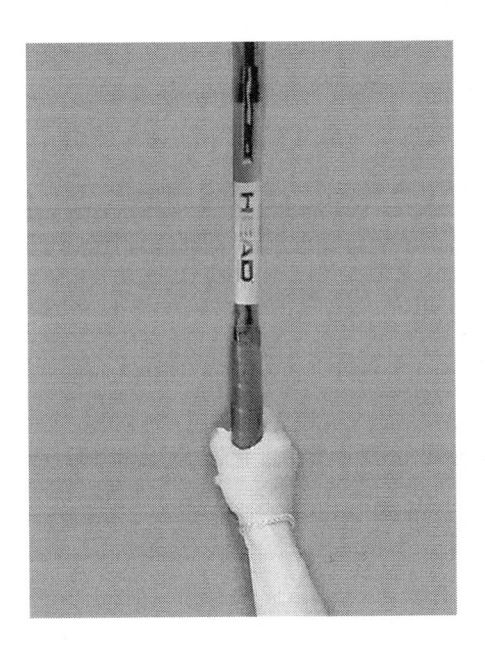

Fig. 1: Continental Grip

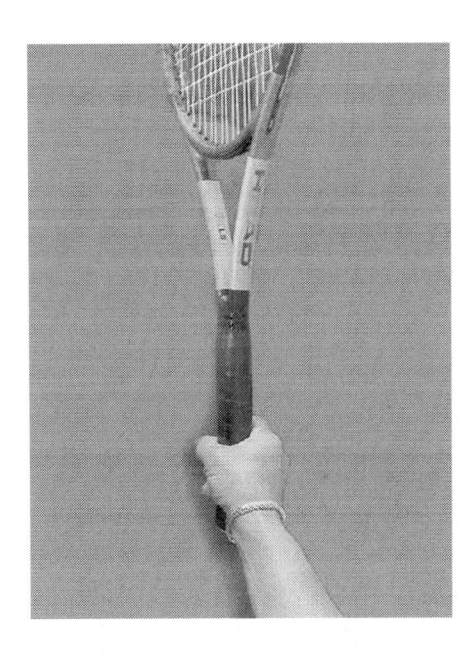

Fig. 2: Here, the racket is tweaked slightly clockwise

Now you're ready to hit some serves—but with two minor adjustments:

1. Aim two feet higher over the net than you normally do.
2. Add a little extra zip!

What you see will bring a tear of joy to even the most calloused flat-server's eye. Your serve will clear the net with a nice margin of safety—and then dive right down into the box. Welcome to a whole new world!

A reliable spin serve is one of the most valuable tennis assets you can own. It allows you to raise your first serve percentage at will, and makes you a stronger player across the board.

For example:

- Your offense will be better because you can be more aggressive with your first serves. You can relax and take more chances with high-risk flat serves when you know you have a nice, heavy spinner to back it up.
- Your defense will be better as well. You'll be able to hit aggressive second serves without worrying about double faults—and that means your second serves will be a lot less attackable.

The harder you hit your serve using the "Grip" trick, the heavier it'll be. A heavy serve has rotation working for it as well as speed—so it grabs the returner's racket and gives it a twist. You *will* need to pronate a little more than usual to direct the ball forward, but it's all good—that extra pronation will add smack to your serve.

Surveys show that most players would rather have a root canal in a frozen field than futz with their grip. But with so many benefits and no down side, there's no reason not to get busy with it. The "Grip" trick gives you *automatic spin*—and that tiny adjustment is all it takes to make the ball do tricks!

THE "FIRST SERVE IN" TRICK

Q: DOUBLE FAULTS ARE KILLING ME! WHAT SHOULD I DO FIRST?

A: The first step is to go for *quantity of first serves* over *quality of first serves*. Remember: No one in the history of tennis has ever double faulted after getting a first serve in!

Double faults are the common colds of tennis: You can't eliminate them, but they certainly don't have to be the death of you. So if chronic double faults are making you sick, this simple prescription is just what the doctor ordered!

THE FIRST SERVE IN RULE

There are two times it's vitally important to get your first serve in—no matter how much speed you have to sacrifice.

1. Get your first serve in whenever you feel you're really starting to lose confidence in your service game.
2. Get your first serve in whenever the score (or momentum) indicates that you can not afford to lose the next point.

When you put a first serve in play you always gain a double advantage: You eliminate the possibility of a double fault, and you keep the pressure squarely on your opponent where it belongs. So stop hammering nails in your own coffin and make the "FSI" rule the first step on your road to recovery.

(If you need a refresher on how to use ball rotation to consistently get your first serve in the box, refer to the "Grip" trick in this chapter.)

THE "SLUMP BUSTER" TRICK

Q: OK . . . I'VE BEEN IN A SERVICE SLUMP FOR ABOUT TWO YEARS NOW! IS THERE ANY WAY I CAN BUST OUT OF IT, OR AM I DOOMED TO LIFE IN HELL?

A: Ah, the dreaded service slump: We've all spent a night in *that* cell, and it's a dark and lonely place! So here's a "Bust Out Of Jail" card you can use whenever you need it.

The quickest way to get back on track is to eliminate as many variables as possible—both vertically and laterally.

VERTICAL RELIEF

- Start by using plenty of net clearance. Then, apply the "Grip" trick and the "Spear" trick in this chapter to make your serves dive into the box.

Great! Over the net and into the court. You're half way there!

LATERAL RELIEF

When you're in a service slump, nothing's more discouraging than seeing an *almost* ace land a couple of inches wide. So re-define your lateral boundaries as follows:

- The best way to reduce the probability of lateral error is to flat out reject the left and right edges of the service box as acceptable targets.
  - Instead, serve straight at your opponent. Aim right for their belly button!

You'll be amazed at the difficulty even good returners experience when the ball is right in on them—whether it's a flat, slice, or kick serve. So forget about nailing the corners or tickling the lines—just keep on pumping in those body shots! And once you make that commitment, it'll be a lot easier to relax and focus on vertical tweaks—such as using the "Spear" trick to make the ball dive into the service box.

But remember—the first step toward service slump relief is always the same:

- You need to reduce your vertical and lateral liability as much as you possibly can.

That's the essence of your getaway plan, and it's as good as gold. So stick to it! If you do, the last sound you'll probably hear is, "Attention all units! Slump Buster has escaped—and is proceeding down Victory Boulevard at a high rate of speed." But it'll be too late, Baby—'cause you're outta there!

THE "ARCHERY" TRICK

Q: HOW DO I GET MY SECOND SERVE IN THE BOX? I'M ALWAYS AFRAID I'LL DOUBLE FAULT!

A: If you miss your first serve, keep things simple on your second serve by applying the same corrections an archer would use.

For an archer, there are only four directional options after a miss: aim higher, aim lower, aim more to the right, or aim more to the left. That's keeping it simple—and that's exactly what you want to do on a second serve.

- Depending on where you missed your first serve, the adjustment(s) you need to make will be obvious. Just like an archer, you'll need to either:

    1. Aim your serve higher over the net.
    2. Aim it lower—but still over the net!
    3. Aim it further to the left.
    4. Aim it further to the right.

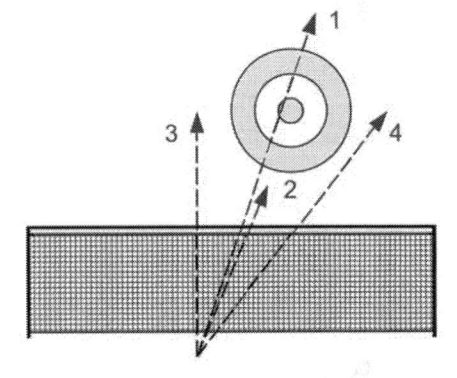

View from the ad (left) court

- If you only need one of those corrections, that's great. And fortunately, the *most* you'll ever need to apply is a combination of two: One for height, plus one for direction.

When you restrict yourself to those simple corrections you eliminate all the non-essentials—and that makes it easy to stay focused on the placement of your serve.

So observe, relax, and make your selection(s)—and then add the power of the spoken word by actually saying to yourself:

- "Aim higher" or "Aim more to the left"—whatever it is you've decided on.

Then, apply your correction boldly, with no fear of failure. Observation, concentration and discipline are the keys that will keep you right on target with your second serves.

THE "FINISH LINE" TRICK – AKA: THE "HIP" TRICK

Q: HOW CAN I MOVE IN MORE QUICKLY WHEN I SERVE-VOLLEY? I HARDLY EVER MAKE IT IN ALL THE WAY TO THE SERVICE LINE FOR MY FIRST SHOT.

A: Transfer more body weight into your serve with a hip thrust.

If you find that you're consistently making your first volley from the backcourt, it's probably because you aren't really shifting your body weight into the court when you serve. Here's a great fix:

Start by putting a ball in your front shorts/panty pocket—the one under your tossing arm. Just stash it there and forget about it for now. Then toe up to the baseline and take a practice toss with a different ball. Toss slightly out in front so that it lands one to two feet inside the court. That will force you to shift your weight forward; if you don't, you won't be able to hit up into the ball the way you need to.

- OK, now that you've got the toss right, take a mental snapshot of exactly what the ball looks like suspended up there.

Then save that image for future reference. If you're disciplined enough to *never* serve-volley unless you see that same picture, it'll be easy for you to win the all-important race *between your front hip and your strings*. (See photos)

The finish line you need to cross in that race is the white ribbon of the baseline.

You're the winner every time the ball you stashed in your front pocket crosses the baseline and enters the court *before* your strings hit the ball in the air!

So start off by tossing an imaginary ball, and while it's rising, shift your weight onto your front leg. Then, thrust your hip forward across the baseline, just as in the photos above. The ball you stashed in your front pocket is your gauge—so look down there as you practice this to make sure your front hip is *really* crossing the baseline in time.

Then, once you're sure you've got your hip thruster working, go ahead and have fun striking some serves. You'll be amazed at how you'll be able to move effortlessly into the court like never before.

Weight transfer is golden, so utilize this trick every time you serve-volley. Just remember to press your front hip across the baseline *before* you swing—exactly like a sprinter pressing their chest across the finish line.

As long as the ball in your front pocket crosses the baseline and enters the court before you strike the serve, then you're off to a winning start. You're ready, willing, and able to move right in to the court to play your best possible serve-volley game!

THE "I CAN SEE CLEARLY NOW" TRICK

Q: MY SERVICE MOTION FEELS ALL CRAMPED AND WEIRD. HOW CAN I SMOOTH IT OUT SO I CAN GET MORE POWER ON MY SERVE?

A: One way is to be sure you lower your tossing arm before you swing.

In the 1970s singer Johnny Nash had a monster hit with the song, "I Can See Clearly Now." In it, he sang:

> *"I can see clearly now the rain has gone*
> *I can see all obstacles in my way.*
> *Gone are the dark clouds that had me blind*
> *It's gonna be a bright, bright sunshiny day."*

That sure sounds like a great feeling, doesn't it—and that's exactly how you're going to feel once you get rid of a major obstacle that could be cramping your service motion.

A very important part of smoothing out your serve is to make sure you completely clear your tossing arm out of the way before you swing up at the ball. Until you do so, that arm actually blocks your ability to rotate forward prior to contact.

Here's a great visualization to help clear things up:

- Pretend there's a magic picture window in front of you as you get ready to serve—magic in the sense that you can serve straight through it without it breaking. The only problem is, it's all covered with soapsuds that are blocking your view of the court!

Heck, that's no good: But luckily, you've got an equally magic squeegee in your tossing hand—and it works fine no matter which way your palm is turned.

- So just before you start to swing up toward the ball, pull your tossing arm straight down to clean off the window in front of you. The trick is to wipe the window all the way down to your waist by the time you hit the ball!

Once you've done that you can freely rotate your upper body into your serve for maximum power—and with your new, smooth motion, you'll be able to sing right along with Johnny Nash:

"I can see clearly now, those suds are gone
There are no obstacles in my way.
I can see clearly now, my serve is smooth
It's gonna be a bright, bright sunshiny day!"

THE "LOCK ON TARGET" TRICK

Q: MY SERVE IS REALLY ERRATIC: SOMETIMES IT'S GREAT, BUT OTHER TIMES IT'S AWFUL! HOW CAN I FIX THAT?

A: If your toss is OK, you're probably not watching the ball closely enough after it leaves your hand.

It's vitally important to lock on target before you deliver the goods!

- So first, lock your eyes on the precise part of the ball you need to strike for the kind of serve you have in mind.
  - That might be the bottom inside corner of the ball—BIC—for a power serve out wide, or more of the outside of the ball for a slice serve. (For more on BIC, see "The Four Quarters" in Key Concepts.)

Then once you're locked on target, just shift your weight onto your front leg for power and whack away!

- But keep in mind that a big bomb is only an asset if you can accurately deliver it to the target!

So even if you don't exactly have a rocket serve, you'll be well served to borrow a concept from the Artillery Corps. They have an old joke that goes something like this . . .

Q: "What do you get when you launch a big shell from a bad canon?"

A: "A swimming pool!"

That means no matter how devastating the payload might be, without an accurate delivery system, all you get is a big old hole in the ground.

So before you swing, always make sure you lock your eyes on whatever part of the ball you intend to hit. That's your ultimate defense against the dreaded SPS (*Swimming Pool Syndrome*).

Once you make it a habit, it'll be a lot easier to deliver your serves right where you want them to go. Then you'll be able to start inflicting some real, consistent damage.

THE "NOSE TO THE BALL" TRICK – SERVES AND OVERHEADS

Q: I MISS AN AWFUL LOT OF SERVES IN THE NET. WHAT'S THE FIRST THING I SHOULD DO TO CURE THAT *FAULT*?

A: Play tall by trying to touch the ball with the tip of your nose just before you swing up at it!

A major cause of chronic "net-itis" is the failure to achieve full extension at contact. This trick will keep you tall and strong—and works equally well for both serves and overheads.

Here's the secret to playing tall . . .

PLAYING TALL ON SERVES

- When you toss, be sure to fully extend your tossing arm high above your head. That will elevate your front shoulder above your hitting shoulder, and prep you for a strong upward rotation into the ball.
    - Then just before you start to swing up at it, try to touch the ball with your nose! That small stretch will guarantee that you're tall and strong at the moment of contact.

PLAYING TALL ON OVERHEADS

- As you set up for your overhead, reach up as high as you can toward the ball with your non-dominant hand, just as in serving. That will elevate your front shoulder above your hitting shoulder, and prep you for a strong upward rotation.
    - Then just before you start to swing up, try to touch the ball with your nose! That small stretch will keep you tall and strong at the moment of contact—and eliminate errors caused by a premature collapse of your upper body.

So if you're sick and tired of missing those two shots in the net, use this trick to get that monkey off your back. You'll see an immediate improvement in the quality of your serves and overheads—and you'll play taller and hit stronger than ever before!

THE "SWISH" TRICK

Q: HOW CAN I ADD SOME SPEED TO MY SERVE? I'M PRETTY SURE I HIT ONE OVER 50 MPH ONCE . . . BUT MY FRIENDS SAY I'M DREAMING!

A: Use the mighty "Swish" trick to generate more racket head speed.

Guess what's at or near the top of most tennis players' wish lists? Almost everyone at every level wants to add speed to their serve. So I'm going to take a wild guess that that's high on your list as well. If your response is "Yes, O Wise One, a thousand times Yes!" then this one's for you.

Here's how it works:

Grab your racket and listen carefully as you swing it through the air at a moderate rate of speed. Hear anything? If not, start adding a little speed to successive swings until you hear a distinct swishing sound. From that point on, you'll notice that the faster you swing, the louder the swish.

- Now you're ready to do the same thing while emulating your regular service motion—and you don't even need to use a ball yet.
  - Starting with a medium speed, swing through your full range of motion—and then gradually increase the speed until you hear a nice swish.

Once you hear it, you're set: Now you have a great audio biofeedback gauge you can use to monitor your racket head speed. And talk about simple . . .

- The louder the swish, the faster the serve!

Obviously physical strength plays a part—but whatever your strength level, more swish means more speed. Tweaks like weight transfer and body rotation will help make your *service cake* rise, but your racket speed is the cake batter itself.

So listen up, and use this reliable early warning system to let you know if your racket head speed is dropping too low. And as for those friends who said you were dreaming? Well guess what: Soon, they'll be the ones dreaming—dreaming of the good old days when it was a lot easier to return your serve!

THE "DON'T LET GO" TRICK

Q: HOW CAN I GET MY SERVICE TOSS UNDER CONTROL? IT'S ALL OVER THE PLACE!

A: Hang onto the ball as long as you can!

Until you develop a consistent toss, serving is always going to be an unpredictable adventure. On days when your toss is good your serve might be very good indeed. But that kind of success is a lot like Tuesday—it only comes around every so often!

So to develop a consistent toss, keep the ball in your tossing hand as long as possible.

- *Do not* open your fingers to release the ball until just prior to full extension, at the very end of your upward lift.
    - It's a vital consideration, *because once the ball leaves your hand, a bad toss drifts farther and farther away from the vertical X-axis!*

The following diagram illustrates how your release point radically affects the final position of the ball in the strike zone.

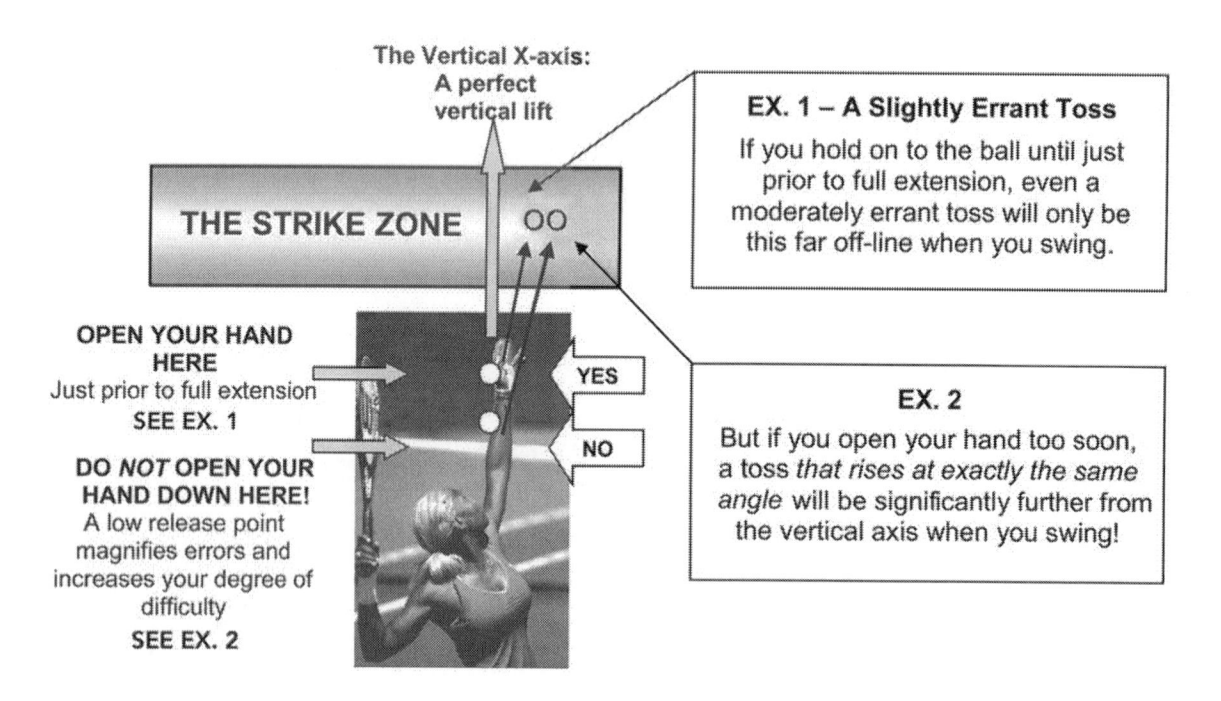

The Vertical X-axis: A perfect vertical lift

THE STRIKE ZONE

EX. 1 – A Slightly Errant Toss
If you hold on to the ball until just prior to full extension, even a moderately errant toss will only be this far off-line when you swing.

OPEN YOUR HAND HERE
Just prior to full extension
SEE EX. 1

YES

NO

DO *NOT* OPEN YOUR HAND DOWN HERE!
A low release point magnifies errors and increases your degree of difficulty
SEE EX. 2

EX. 2
But if you open your hand too soon, a toss *that rises at exactly the same angle* will be significantly further from the vertical axis when you swing!

Remember, the sooner you open your fingers, the further off-line the ball will be when it finally reaches the strike zone. So always hang on to the ball until your arm is almost fully extended. *Hang on as if your serve depends on it—because it does!*

With a little practice you'll soon see a huge improvement—and you'll stop *breaking yourself with bad tosses*. This one's oh, so simple: For a consistent toss that will make it a lot easier to hold serve, just "Don't Let Go!" too soon.

THE "POT OF GOLD" TRICK

Q: HOW CAN I STILL SERVE EFFECTIVELY WHEN I GET ALL NERVOUS AND TIGHT?

A: Unless you're the coolest cucumber that ever grew in a garden, sooner or later, *you are going to get nervous and tight!* But never fear—you can still serve effectively as long as you keep your racket head moving *after* you hit the ball.

According to Celtic legend, there's a pot of gold at the end of every rainbow. In this case, the pot of gold is a consistent, fully functional serve—one you can count on even when you've got a bad case of the yips.

The yips are all about stress. Stress almost always inhibits your ability to think clearly and act quickly, and can inject a hitch into even the smoothest stroke. It's always ugly, but nowhere is it more glaring and painful than when it bites you right in your service motion—that most naked of all actions.

- A great way to beat the service yips is to make sure you "Follow the rainbow." The rainbow in this situation is the arc that runs from the point where you strike the ball, *all the way to the end of the natural finish of your service motion.*
  - For most players (except on a kick serve) that point will be below waist level—across your body and on the outside of the leg *opposite* your hitting arm.

The exact finish can vary from player to player, and definitely varies according to the specific type of serve. But wherever it happens to be for you, that's the end of your rainbow.

So when the yips start nipping at your confidence, remember to keep your racket head moving all the way to the finish. That's where you'll find your pot of gold—the ability to serve effectively even when you're stressed to the max!

6
RETURN OF SERVE MAGIC

QUESTIONS	TRICKS	
I have to break serve right now! Where do I start?	*Mighty Oak*	120
It's a huge point and I don't know what kind of serve they're going to hit. Help!	*Batter With Two Strikes*	121
They're killing me with their favorite serve. What can I do?	*Denial*	122
I totally go into victim mode when I'm facing a tough server. How can I realign my mind, if you would be so kind?	*Predator*	123

THE "MIGHTY OAK" TRICK

Q: I HAVE TO BREAK SERVE RIGHT NOW! WHERE DO I START?

A: This trick is the mightiest oak in the forest of Return of Serve. So rely on its strength whenever it's now or never.

- Unless your opponent double faults, there's only one way to break them: You have to start by getting their serve back in play.

Sure, it's as obvious as an elephant in a pear tree; but obvious can be tricky, and has a naughty way of slipping under the radar. So just for insurance sake, make the following declaration as you prepare to return serve:

- "I must get this return in play—over the net and into the court!"

There's just no getting around that necessity. Barring the gift of double faults, no one in the history of tennis has *ever* broken serve without getting the return in play.

- So elevate the goal of hitting a successful return to priority number one. That total commitment on your part will empower you in doing whatever it takes to pull it off—be it stretch, stab, spear, flail, beg, hope or plead.

Here, especially, keep in mind that technical considerations take a back seat to utility. Pretty is as pretty does—and when the game's on the line, the only ugly returns are the ones you miss!

So when you absolutely have to break serve, take shelter under the "Mighty Oak." Declare your intention early—"Over the net and into the court!"—and then focus 100 percent on getting the ball in play. Once you do that, you've got a fighting chance—and you're off and running toward that crucial break!

THE "BATTER WITH TWO STRIKES" TRICK

Q: IT'S A HUGE POINT AND I DON'T KNOW WHAT KIND OF SERVE THEY'RE GOING TO HIT. HELP!

A: If they've shown you an effective flat serve (a fastball), watch out for that pitch first—because it affords you the least amount of time to react.

Facing a versatile server is always tough, especially when it's game point. So use the following visualization to help you stay focused:

- Pretend you're a batter facing a two-strike count, and your team is down to its final out. In that situation your number one challenge is to avoid a strikeout!

Your first line of defense in that regard should be to bisect their available serving angles in case they fire a fastball. That's because if you cheat away from the bisector, you'll risk getting burned on the other side of the box.

YOUR FIRST LINE OF DEFENSE – THE BISECTOR

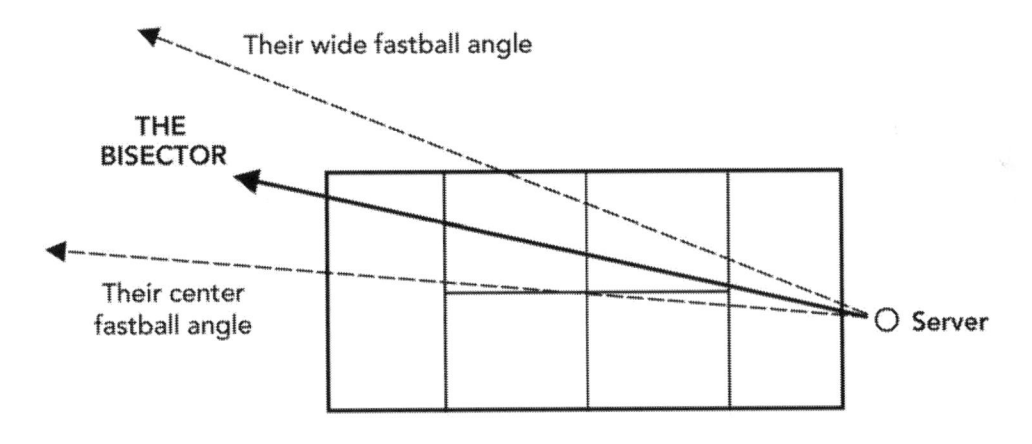

YOUR SECOND LINE OF DEFENSE – ALERTNESS!

There's no substitute for alertness! So be mentally prepared to sprint like the dickens if they hit a slice or a kick serve. Luckily, curve balls and change-ups come in more slowly—and as long as you aren't napping you should be able to react in time.

So play smart, batter. Think fastball first; but stay alert in case they throw you something tricky. When you're on the short end of a two-strike count, focus and alertness are everything!

THE "DENIAL" TRICK

Q: THEY'RE KILLING ME WITH THEIR FAVORITE SERVE. WHAT CAN I DO?

A: Refuse to let them hold serve the easy way. Make it your mission to deny them their favorite target—no matter how much you have to overplay!

Most players have a favorite serve, and they'll keep right on punishing you with it until you give them a darn good reason to stop. So if they're inflicting serious damage, you might have to bite the bullet and take radical action to make them switch to Plan B. Plan B is often significantly less effective—which is probably why it's not Plan A!

So once you've figured out how they like to do their dirt, your job is simple:

- Just stand wherever you need to to deny them their favorite option! And go extreme as necessary—no matter how silly it might look.

For example:

1. If they're hurting you with their untouchable slice serve, move your ready position way over toward that side of the box so you can cover it.
2. If they're beating you with a flat serve up the center tee, take up a ready position way over toward that side of the box.

Sure, that will leave you more exposed to a serve out wide—but at least you'll force them to prove they're versatile enough to take advantage of the opportunity.

- If they're unable to adjust with a strong countermeasure, then your evil work is almost done! Just continue to overplay in the appropriate direction—and watch them crumple like the paper tiger you know they are.

This trick is absolutely essential whenever you have a breakpoint in hand—but you don't have to wait until then to use it! You can use it to test the waters anytime you smell trouble, just to see how your opponent reacts.

- Nobody likes being forced off their game plan early. So if you shrink their favorite target area they're much more likely to start pressing—and therefore much more likely to start missing!

So up the ante—*and challenge them for that target area!* As they say on the East side, it's all about "Who's gonna be the boss of who." Hey, they're not the boss of you—so get busy and prove to your opponent that denial can be a beautiful thing!

THE "PREDATOR" TRICK

Q: I TOTALLY GO INTO VICTIM MODE WHEN I'M FACING A TOUGH SERVER. HOW CAN I REALIGN MY MIND, IF YOU WOULD BE SO KIND?

A: Rather than think of yourself as a victim on the receiving end of a tough serve, think of yourself as an eager predator ready to pounce all over it!

When you want to make an impression on the server, it's awfully tempting to use a full wind-up—the same one you use when you want to blast a groundstroke winner. But what if the serve comes in faster than you expected?

- In that case, a huge wind-up will wind up messing up your shot!

A much more efficient option is the predator return—which is a powerful application of the "Less is more" principle. It enables you to punish the server by means of a quick *turn and strike* that rockets the ball back before they know what hit them.

There are two key elements to a perfect predator pounce:

1. As soon as the ball leaves your opponent's strings, show *your* strings to the ball. All it takes is a short backswing and a quick hip and shoulder turn to the appropriate side.

2. Then drive through the ball with a quick, sharp strike. Aim for the bottom inside corner (BIC) if possible: Low to high for topspin, vice versa for underspin. (For more on BIC, see "The Four Quarters" in Key Concepts.)

Bear in mind that you don't necessarily need the wraparound topspin finish you might normally use during a rally. Your primary focus should just be on the strike itself.

- So think lean and mean. The predator is sleek and compact—and it's most effective when you keep it short, sweet and deadly!

Elegance has been defined as "The maximum possible output from the minimum possible input"—and certainly, it's a lovely expression of *less is more* in action. So dare to be elegant with a predator return by substituting a quick *turn and strike* for a big wind-up. When you do that, you can expect to do a lot more breaking with a lot less effort—and that's elegant indeed!

7
VOLLEY MAGIC

QUESTIONS

Introduction – Over Or Under?

Stepping into my volleys isn't working so well. What's wrong?

A lot of my underspin volleys just kind of sit there—with "Pass me!" written all over them. How can I add some zip and penetration?

I'll be honest—sometimes I get a little bit scared up at the net. How can a cowardly lion like me conquer this leaning stuff?

Low forehand volleys give me trouble, and I often wind up netting them. What can I do to change that?

TRICKS

Introduction To The Volley	128
Lean On Me – Part 1: There's A New Kid In Town	129
Lean On Me – Part 2: Zip It!	130
Lean On Me – Part 3: Fear Not!	132
Catch It	133

I've heard I should always take a check step on my way to the net. But *where* exactly should I take it?	*Stop And Go Find – Part 1*	136
When should I *never* take a check step?	*Stop And Go Find – Part 2*	137
What's the simplest way to improve the accuracy of my volley placements?	*Video-Cam*	138
I'm always getting caught in the wrong grip in midcourt. What's the best way to prepare for the unexpected?	*Helmet*	139
I see lots of pros ripping topspin volleys. Dare I try it, or is it out of my league?	*Swing Away*	140
Some of my volleys are so sloppy and weak. How can I put more of them away?	*Kung Fu*	141
I want to be more aggressive on my volleys—but not at the expense of consistency. How can I do that and still maintain my accuracy?	*Shuffleboard*	142
I'm often late on my volleys. How can I get my racket ready in time?	*Fingernails*	143
Sometimes I take too big a backswing on my traditional underspin volleys and wind up spraying the ball. How can I fix that?	*Hold That Wrist*	144

Can you give me a good visualization to help make me a more proactive volleyer?	*Megaphone*	146
I'm getting killed in rapid exchanges at the net. What's the best way to handle quick, consecutive volleys?	*Zorro*	147

INTRODUCTION TO THE VOLLEY – OVER OR UNDER?

Back in the twentieth century, the underspin volley ruled. Occasionally a player would swing over a volley with topspin—but that choice would invariably elicit an immediate cry of "Don't try that at home!" from the commentators. That's because wood rackets were heavy and had a small sweet spot—so a big swing was often a challenging choice. But boy, have times changed. Thanks to the maneuverability and power of lighter modern rackets, the mighty topspin volley has become an integral part of the game.

THE OVER – The Swinging Topspin Volley

Once a questionable choice, it's now a totally live option—a tremendous asset that every player should own.

- It's as fun and exciting as a monster overhead, or a slam-dunk in basketball—and it's extremely easy to learn and execute. (See the "Swing Away" trick in this chapter.)

Keep in mind, however, that the smashmouth swing volley *is not a substitute for,* nor will it ever replace, the more versatile underspin volley—just as the slam-dunk in basketball will never replace the more versatile lay-up.

THE UNDER – The Classic Underspin Volley

Though less flashy, the traditional underspin volley will always remain the foundation of the volley game, and for that reason it is the main focus of this chapter. Tried and true for generations, its importance is in no way diminished by the ascension of the topspin volley.

- For one thing, it's impossible to hit a topspin *drop volley*—you need to use underspin to make that beauty! And then there's the time consideration:
  - Reaction is everything in high-speed volleying, and often there's just no time to wield a swinging broadsword. When milliseconds count, a rapier underspin volley can be a real lifesaver—and every bit as deadly as its flashier sibling!

The bottom line is, modern volleying is all about options—and versatility rules. As Don Meredith once said during a Monday Night Football telecast, "If you've got one trick, you've got no tricks!" So have fun and keep 'em guessing. Over or under, sidespin or no spin—more than ever before, it's your choice!

THE "LEAN ON ME" TRICK – PART 1: THERE'S A NEW KID IN TOWN

Q: STEPPING INTO MY VOLLEYS ISN'T WORKING SO WELL. WHAT'S WRONG?

A: It's not you, it's the times—or should I say, the lack of time!

The game of tennis is faster now than it's ever been—and that can create problems if you *always* use the time-honored technique of stepping into a volley.

- Stepping is only effective when you have enough time to implement a two-part process.
    1. First, you have to assess where the ball is headed.
    2. Then—*and only then*—can you step toward it!

Obviously, that's no problem on a slow or medium paced shot—but try stepping into a Serena Williams forehand when she's all set up about twenty feet in front of you. Now you've got a big problemo: No fun-o, and probably no hope-o!

The fact is, each and every day players are raising the power game to new heights. They're hitting the ball scary fast, and their rockets have exposed *mandatory* stepping for what it is—a hopelessly outdated technique for dealing with that kind of pace.

No wonder your old technique fails you sometimes! What you need is a brand new paradigm that's much better suited to the blistering pace of modern tennis.

- In order to gain the maximum edge in the 21st century, you need to understand and apply the magic of *leaning into a volley* as opposed to *stepping into a volley*.

So let me take this opportunity to introduce you to "Leaning." He's the new kid in town—and someone you definitely want to know!

> *"Lean on me, when you're not strong*
> *I'll be your friend, I'll help you carry on . . . "*
>
> ~ Bill Withers

Leaning is the bright future of the volley game—a simple, elegant, and effective way to maximize your efficiency on any volley, from a puffball floater to a monster pass. In part two of this trick, you'll discover everything you need to know about your new friend.

THE "LEAN ON ME" TRICK – Part 2: ZIP IT!

Q: A LOT OF MY UNDERSPIN VOLLEYS JUST KIND OF SIT THERE—WITH "PASS ME!" WRITTEN ALL OVER THEM. HOW CAN I ADD SOME ZIP AND PENETRATION?

A: The only way to get more zip on your volleys is to increase your racket head speed—and there are only two ways to do that:

1. SWING HARDER: You'll definitely get more zip—but you'll also increase your risk of error.
2. SHIFT YOUR BODY WEIGHT TOWARD THE BALL: That'll give you the extra zip you want without any downside!

Leaning into volleys is a special application of the "Collapse It" trick in Body Magic. There, you learn that the quickest way to move laterally is to lean hard in the direction you want to go, while simultaneously collapsing that leg. Here's how to use that same principle to add more zip to your volleys:

- When you assume your ready position, lift your heels a fraction of an inch off the ground. Then, as your opponent starts to move their strings forward into the ball, lean forward just a wee bit.

From that point on, everything from your waist down will take care of itself!

- If their shot comes straight at you, you're golden—just continue to lean forward, and the ball will pop off your strings like you won't believe!
- And if the ball is wide left or right, no worries! You can move laterally in a flash just by collapsing the appropriate leg.

Remember, the problem with old school stepping is that it's *by necessity reactive*—because you have to wait for the ball to leave your opponent's strings before you move toward it! That element of reactivity can make for a pretty weak response against an incoming rocket.

- Leaning, on the other hand, is totally proactive—because you shift your balance forward *before the ball leaves your opponent's strings.*
  - That's why as a leaner, you'll get to a lot of balls that zoom right past a stepper! It's the natural evolution of stepping—tailor-made for high velocity tennis.

Hopefully, these insights will inspire you to lean right into the future of the volley game. But if it still seems a little too radical or far out of your comfort zone—or if you just flat out hate trying anything new—the following two tricks are probably your best bet.

THE "WOODY" TRICK

Be *absolutely sure* your opponent is playing with a wood racket—preferably one that's strung extra, extra tight! In that case you'll probably have plenty of time to step into all your volleys.

THE "MASOCHIST" TRICK

Have a deep and inordinate affection for dishing up more of those weak volleys that scream, "Pass me—now!" Because unless you're working the "Woody Trick," you should expect some mighty cruel treatment up at the net.

But all kidding aside, the best way to get the results you want is to start kickin' it with the "Lean On Me" trick. The old "Step into your volleys!" commandment is strictly a situational play now. It's still fine advice for slow to medium paced balls—but there sure aren't as many of those as there were back in the day.

The bottom line is, time marches on; and all advice, no matter how cherished, must evolve with the game or perish. So be brave, little cowpoke! Whenever you want to add more zip to your volleys just remind yourself:

> "I can wait and be late,
> or I can lean and be mean!"

THE "LEAN ON ME" TRICK – Part 3: FEAR NOT!

Q: I'LL BE HONEST—SOMETIMES I GET A LITTLE BIT SCARED UP AT THE NET. HOW CAN A COWARDLY LION LIKE ME CONQUER THIS LEANING STUFF?

A: By recognizing your fears for the paper tigers they are!

Players who feel uncomfortable about leaning into their volleys usually voice one or both of the following concerns:

1. "I'm afraid I'll get passed if I commit to leaning toward the ball."
2. "I'm afraid I'll wind up eating a 100 mile an hour fuzz sandwich!"

While those are understandable concerns, they're largely unwarranted—so let's dispel those phantoms once and for all.

PAPER TIGER # 1: "I JUST KNOW I'M GOING TO GET PASSED!"

- If you lean toward the ball as your opponent starts to move their strings forward and you get passed, guess what? It wasn't *because* of your proactive lean that you got passed—*you simply got passed in spite of it!*

The hard truth is, there's no defense against a well-placed passing shot: If it's out of your reach, it's out of your reach. And playing *reactively* certainly won't help; that will just cause you to get passed by an even wider margin.

PAPER TIGER # 2: "I JUST KNOW I'M GOING TO GET HIT BY AN INCOMING ROCKET!"

Believe it or not, you're actually *less likely* to get hit when you lean forward proactively! Here's why:

- The act of leaning forward *in and of itself* puts you in a heightened state of alertness.
  - That's because when you lean, your natural reflex to catch your balance kicks right in—the same natural reflex you developed as a toddler while first learning to walk.

For that brief "Whoops!" instant, you're razor sharp for whatever needs to be done next—which is a huge plus if your opponent's shot is so hot you need to just lean out of the way and let it whiz on by. In that case—well, that's one for them . . . Grrrrr! But more often than not, you'll find that you're all over their passing shots like white on rice.

So fear not! At the very least, leaning will give you a fighting chance of getting your racket on some really tough shots. And as your confidence increases so will your success—and before you know it, you'll be attacking your volleys like the mighty king of the jungle you really are.

THE "CATCH IT" TRICK

Q: LOW FOREHAND VOLLEYS GIVE ME TROUBLE, AND I OFTEN WIND UP NETTING THEM. WHAT CAN I DO TO CHANGE THAT?

A: Always use an open, beveled racket face—and set an angle of bevel the instant the ball leaves your opponent's strings!

Beginners are often reluctant to use bevel because they're afraid they'll pop the ball up and give their opponent an easy put-away. But there's just no doubt about it:

- Bevel is Queen when it comes to mastering the traditional underspin volley.

An open, beveled racket face is a lifesaver on low volleys. It provides a natural upward trajectory to help clear the net, and automatically imparts underspin to keep the ball low after it bounces. So curry Her Majesty's good favor by learning to move your beveled palm toward the ball.

Although you *can* volley in any grip, I highly recommend Continental. Granted, some famous world-class coaches vary in their opinions, but on this point I agree wholeheartedly with the outstanding tennis educator Peter Burwash. The greatest gift you can give yourself in regard to volleying is to use Continental grip, end of story.

- That's because in Continental, *the angle of your palm and the angle of your strings is always identical!* So once you set the angle of your palm, you're good: That will be the precise angle of your strings at contact.

The following *toss and catch* exercises will give you a great feel for volleying with a beveled racket face.

EXERCISE 1: Start by using your *hitting hand* to toss a ball a couple of feet into the air, and then catch it at chest level with a flat palm. Repeat until comfortable.

EXERCISE 2: Now toss again—but as soon as you release the ball, (A) swing your tossing hand a few inches out to the side and then (B) quickly bring it back under the ball for the catch. (See Fig. 1)

Figure 1

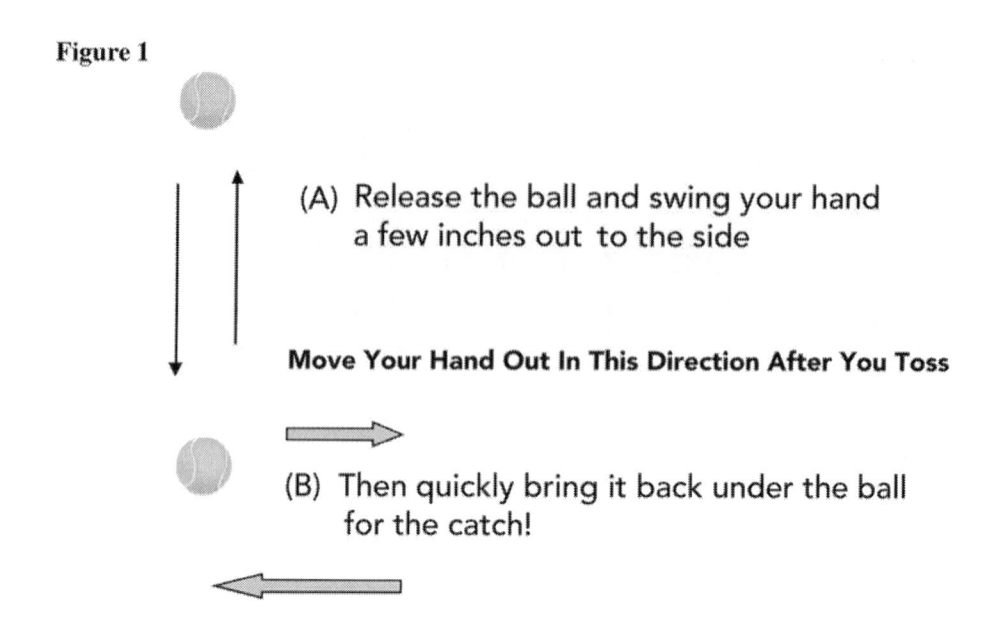

(A) Release the ball and swing your hand a few inches out to the side

Move Your Hand Out In This Direction After You Toss

(B) Then quickly bring it back under the ball for the catch!

Move Your Flat Palm Right Back Here

Be sure to take your time with Exercise 2. You'll want to repeat it until you're completely comfortable with it, because it's the foundation of a pro volley!

EXERCISE 3: Now you're ready to add the final ingredient—the almighty bevel!

- After each toss (as per Fig. 1) you're now going to tilt the bottom edge of your hand downward about 45 degrees *before you bring it back in to catch the ball.* (See Fig. 2)

Figure 2

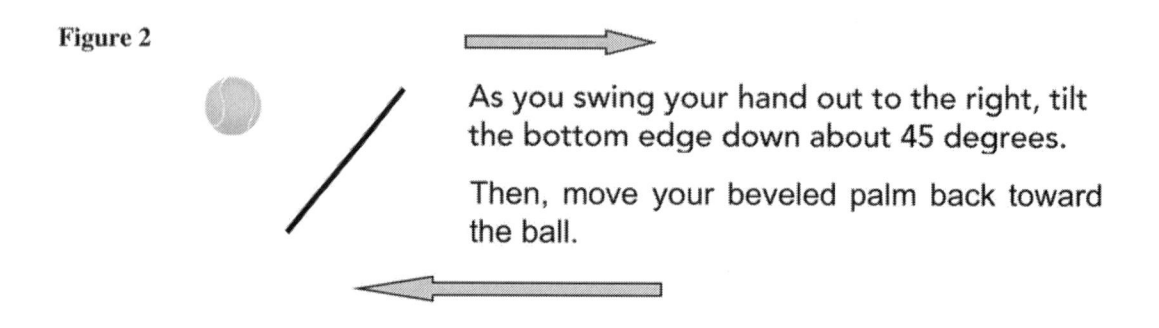

As you swing your hand out to the right, tilt the bottom edge down about 45 degrees.

Then, move your beveled palm back toward the ball.

- That's your volley bevel! Once you set it, you're ready to play forehand volleys like a pro, just as in this photo.

As I mentioned previously, Continental grip is your ideal choice for underspin volleys. Initially, in ready position—with your hand in front of your bellybutton, racket tip forward and up about forty-five degrees—the inward curve of your hitting-hand wrist may feel awkward. But do soldier on; you'll get used to it quickly, and it's so worth it! Once you show your beveled palm to the ball Continental feels beautifully natural, and you can easily monitor the precise angle of your strings.

But whatever grip you use, remember that on low balls, bevel rules. So keep your motion short and sweet and just move your beveled palm into the ball. That's a great way to turn your net losses into net gains!

THE "STOP AND GO FIND" TRICK – Part 1

Q: I'VE HEARD I SHOULD ALWAYS TAKE A CHECK STEP ON MY WAY TO THE NET. BUT *WHERE* EXACTLY SHOULD I TAKE IT?

A: The answer is much more a matter of time than of place. If you focus on *when,* the where will take care of itself!

- As you head toward the net, it's intuitive to advance as far as you can as fast as you can. But that can cause problems, because it's virtually impossible to change direction if you have your weight on the wrong foot when your opponent hits their shot.

That's where a check step comes in—and that's why *when* should be your primary concern.

THE WHEN RULE

- No matter where you are en route to the net, it's smart to take a check step just as your opponent starts to move their strings toward the ball.

That's because no matter how clever you are, you can never be sure where their shot is going. Heck, sometimes *they're* not even sure! So unless you intend to guess, always take a check step. Otherwise, you could get wrong-footed and passed by a ball that isn't all that far away from you.

- Remember, a check step is a *brief pause* in a balanced position that allows you to (A) evaluate what needs to be done next, and (B) move quickly to intercept the ball. (See "My Checkered Path" in Key Concepts)

Now, let's factor in the *where* consideration.

THE WHERE RULE

- As long as your opponent is *not yet within hitting range of the ball,* there's no reason to take a check step until you arrive at ideal volley position, halfway between the service line and the net.
  - That's the "where" part of the equation. Once you're there—paused and on balance—you're in great position to respond to either a passing shot or a lob.

Obviously, the where consideration is an important one—but it should be equally obvious that the "When Rule" rules! So armed with that knowledge, it's tally-ho to the net—and until either the When or the Where rule kicks in, just keep right on coming in!

THE "STOP AND GO FIND" TRICK – Part 2

Q: WHEN SHOULD I *NEVER* TAKE A CHECK STEP?

A: Never take a check step if you're totally committed to gambling—either by choice or by necessity. In those situations, an all or nothing burst is your best bet.

Let's take a look at both circumstances:

GAMBLING BY CHOICE

- If you elect to make a strong move—either to poach, or to cover a particular area of the court—take off and go for all you're worth!

If it's part of a pre-arranged doubles strategy, you should trust your partner implicitly to cover behind you. Your part of the bargain is simply to go all out to cover the agreed upon area—without fail and as quickly as possible.

GAMBLING BY NECESSITY

- If you believe your court position is so compromised that your best chance is to guess and anticipate your opponent's shot, then put it in high gear and get going! Once again, forget about taking a check step: Just run like heck toward wherever you expect the ball to go.

In either circumstance, it's obvious that *not taking a check step* will allow you to get where you're going sooner. So run like the wind and have fun—and if you do get burned, well, "No worries mate!" You just took a flyer and lost.

But big deal! Anybody can play it safe all the time, and life's too short not to take chances. So give it 100 percent whenever you decide to roll those laughing bones. If you guess right, it's Tupelo honey—and the harder you have to run for the ball, the sweeter it is!

THE "VIDEO-CAM" TRICK

Q: WHAT'S THE SIMPLEST WAY TO IMPROVE THE ACCURACY OF MY VOLLEY PLACEMENTS?

A: If you've ever said to yourself, "I would be so much more willing to come to the net if only my volleys were a little more precise," then this trick's for you.

- A great way to improve the accuracy of your volleys is to keep your racket face on line with your target *for a split second after contact.*

Imagine you've installed a tiny video-cam lens right in the center of your racket strings to record the flight path of your shots. In order to really capture that, you'll need to keep the lens pointed in the direction of your target for at least a split second after contact.

- Granted, when you use an open, beveled racket face for an underspin volley, your video-cam lens will actually point *above your target* rather than directly at it. But as long as you don't let the lens look off to the left or right, the lateral accuracy of both your video coverage and your volleys will be equally true.

So start your video masterpiece today, and get ready to have big fun at the net. Not only will you dazzle your friends with your newfound accuracy—you might even get to hear them shout, "Film at 11:00!" when you volley!

THE "HELMET" TRICK

Q: I'M ALWAYS GETTING CAUGHT IN THE WRONG GRIP IN MIDCOURT. WHAT'S THE BEST WAY TO PREPARE FOR THE UNEXPECTED?

A: The ultimate defense against the unexpected is Continental grip!

Before you can get from the baseline to the net you have to cross the Bermuda Triangle of the midcourt, where you never know what type of shot you'll need to play next. So unless you're determined to join the countless ships, planes and points that have been lost there, a little preparation is in order.

- The surest way to prepare for a wide range of possibilities is to don the magic safety helmet of *Continental grip* prior to making your advance!
  - The fact that it's a great grip for volleys, half volleys, and overheads makes it an ideal choice for dealing with anything your opponent throws at you.

For example, when you come in behind your serve or hit an approach shot from a moderately deep position, you never know what kind of midcourt shot you'll need to hit first. It could be a volley, a half volley, or if they lob, an overhead.

- But no worries—as long as you put on your safety helmet the instant you venture into midcourt, you'll be ready-spaghetti!

The one exception in which it's fine to set some *other* grip before you enter midcourt is when your opponent volunteers a short ball while you're still in the backcourt or deeper. In that case, your next shot will almost certainly be a groundstroke—so it makes perfect sense to advance in whatever grip you intend to use for that shot.

But then, as soon as you complete your shot, remember to don your Continental helmet again. As long as it's on, you'll be armed, ready and dangerous—and you'll never get caught in the wrong grip again!

THE "SWING AWAY" TRICK

Q: I SEE LOTS OF PROS RIPPING TOPSPIN VOLLEYS. DARE I TRY IT, OR IS IT OUT OF MY LEAGUE?

A: Don't just try it . . . make it a dynamic part of your arsenal!

The most exciting volley innovation in the early 21st century is the emergence of the swing volley as a commonplace kill shot. The maneuverability and power of modern rackets make it as easy as it is deadly—so by all means, join the "Swing Away" club!

Why is it so easy?

- Because you use the same technique you use for your topspin groundstrokes! The only difference is you hit the ball *before* it bounces.

All you have to do to make it a reliable part of your game is incorporate three fundamental groundstroke tricks:

1. Use the "Ramp" trick in Groundstroke Magic for net clearance. The more the ball drops on you, the more you need to *hit uphill* for safe net clearance.

2. Add a little BIC for control and accuracy. (See the "Four Quarters" in Key Concepts.)

3. Finally, use the "Finish It" trick in Groundstroke Magic to bring your shot down into the court.

Amazingly, that's all there is to it. So start swinging those close matches your way with your awesome swing volleys. Hard? Hardly! The only *hard* is the hard time you'll be giving your opponents!

THE "KUNG FU" TRICK

Q: SOME OF MY VOLLEYS ARE SO SLOPPY AND WEAK. HOW CAN I PUT MORE OF THEM AWAY?

A: Apply a little Kung Fu magic to add penetrating karate-like power to your volleys!

There's a type of karate chop that stops just past the point of impact and then snaps back in the opposite direction—and you can apply that same action to your volleys to increase both zip and accuracy.

Use the following sequence to get a feel for it:

- Show your strings to the ball nice and early, and then move them forward *a maximum of six inches into the volley.*
- Then, stop the forward motion of your hand/racket unit right at the point of impact.
- Finally, while maintaining a nice firm wrist, snap your entire hand/racket unit backward a couple of inches from there.

That *stop and reverse* action makes it impossible to overswing—so you're much less likely to hit a sloppy volley.

Now you're ready to use this in combat, and the following three basics will help keep you right on track.

Whenever possible:

1. Make contact well out in front of your body.
2. Keep your wrist firm, and below the level of the ball.
3. Stop the forward motion of your racket abruptly, about four inches past the point of contact. I'm saying four inches so you won't go eight inches—six inches is often just about right.

This trick is a beautiful application of the adage "Less is more." When you minimize your motion that way you'll add Kung-fu power to your volleys—and maximize your success at the net!

THE "SHUFFLEBOARD" TRICK

Q: I WANT TO BE MORE AGGRESSIVE ON MY VOLLEYS—BUT NOT AT THE EXPENSE OF CONSISTENCY. HOW CAN I DO THAT AND STILL MAINTAIN MY ACCURACY?

A: The key to linear accuracy is simple:

- Keep your strings on-line with your target—*both during and after contact*—with no sideways slashing!

Outdoor shuffleboard provides a great model. In that game players use a cue stick to slide a weighted disc down the court—and the only direction they push is dead straight ahead!

- That same straight-ahead motion on a volley can do wonders for your accuracy, because it creates a substantial head-on collision with the ball.

Sure, we all know slicer-dicers who carve the ball with stunning success—but there's a daunting challenge in using that type of motion:

- Your timing has to be nearly perfect, because when you slash, there's only a brief instant during which your strings are both (A) actually on the ball and (B) moving directly toward your target.

Now obviously, that's asking a lot when you're faced with anything other than a routine shot. Fortunately, the shuffleboard model will help you maintain accuracy on all your volleys—even when your timing is a little bit off.

- In moving your strings straight out toward your target, you maximize the duration of contact—and that's a huge help if you're either a little early or a little late. As long as your strings are moving forward at contact, you've still got a good shot at a good shot!

So when accuracy is your primary concern, think shuffleboard—and keep your strings on-line with your target *both during and after contact.* Once you see how effective it is, you'll gain all the confidence you need to take your volley game straight to the next level.

THE "FINGERNAILS" TRICK

Q: I'M OFTEN LATE ON MY VOLLEYS. HOW CAN I GET MY RACKET READY IN TIME?

A: Usually, the closer you are to the net, the less time you have to react—which means *something* needs to happen instantly. So when the ball leaves your opponent's strings, *immediately* rotate your shoulders toward the flight path, and then thrust out the bottom edge of your hand to meet it!

PLAN A: YOUR BEST CASE TIME SCENARIO

If you have sufficient time, you can both rotate and thrust.

- First, rotate your shoulders and bellybutton in the appropriate direction for either a forehand or backhand volley.

- Then immediately push out the bottom edge of your hand toward the ball. *Lead with your fingernails if it's a forehand, or the knuckles of your fist if it's a backhand.*

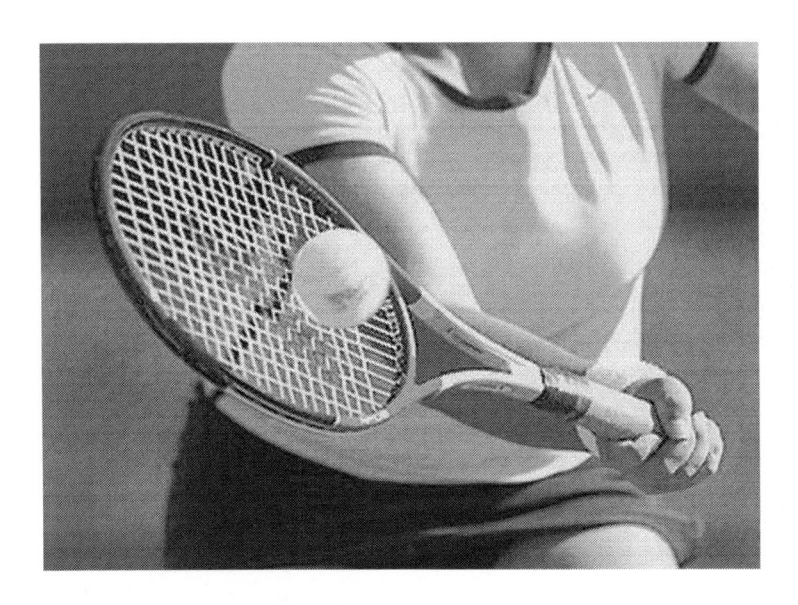

For a forehand volley, simply tilt your palm up and lead the thrust with your fingernails, as in the photo above. If it's a backhand volley, tilt your palm down and lead with your pinkie and ring finger knuckles, while keeping a nice firm wrist.

PLAN B: YOUR WORST CASE TIME SCENARIO

Just Thrust!

- If there's no time to rotate, just make a quick, hard push out toward the ball with the bottom edge of your hand—*leading with your pinkie fingernail or knuckle.*

In both cases—forehand and backhand—something great happens every time you thrust the bottom edge of your hand toward the ball.

- That rapid forward thrust—in conjunction with the inertia of your stationary racket—*automatically presents your strings to the ball.* That can make all the difference between being late on a volley and being ready in time.

So push out the bottom edge of your hand to take maximum advantage of whatever time is available. It's one of the few instances in polite company where being pushy almost always leads to success.

THE "HOLD THAT WRIST" TRICK

Q: SOMETIMES I TAKE TOO BIG A BACKSWING ON MY TRADITIONAL UNDERSPIN VOLLEYS AND WIND UP SPRAYING THE BALL. HOW CAN I FIX THAT?

A: The only problem with a big backswing is that it takes a certain amount of time to execute. Therein lies the rub . . .

- Early contact is a key element of an effective underspin volley—and you can't possibly make contact out in front if your racket is still back there behind you somewhere! Fortunately, there's an easy way to learn a more abbreviated and effective motion.

Start by holding your racket in Continental grip in a relaxed, ready volley position: Hand in front of your bellybutton, racket tip forward and up about forty-five degrees.

- Once you're set in that ready position with your racket strings perpendicular to the ground, you should be able to see only the top edge of your frame. If you can see the strings on either side, rotate your forearm until they disappear.

Now it goes without saying that a good volleyer always supports their racket with their non-dominant hand, usually at the throat. But in order to permanently kill the urge to use a big backswing, you need to temporarily take a different tack.

- First, take your helping hand *off the frame.* Then, turn your palm up and close that hand gently around your dominant wrist.

Now you're ready to play a series of volleys, all without releasing your hold on your wrist. And as long as you continue to hold onto your wrist, your volley motion will by necessity stay nice and compact.

- As the ball approaches keep the butt of your racket in front of your bellybutton—while simultaneously turning your hips and shoulders in the appropriate direction to present your strings to the ball.

- And as you turn, tilt the palm of your hitting hand *upward a little* to create bevel and net clearance for a forehand volley, or *downward a little* for a backhand volley. Then, go for that sweet early contact way out in front of you!

Once you get comfortable with that extremely controlled volley action, you can reposition your non-dominant hand back to its normal support position on the frame. Then just continue using your new, minimalist *turn preparation* on all your subsequent volleys. You'll be thrilled to discover that as you lose that pesky exaggerated backswing, you gain control and accuracy—and before you know it, those wild days of whacko-smacko will be just a fuzzy memory!

THE "MEGAPHONE" TRICK

Q: CAN YOU GIVE ME A GOOD VISUALIZATION TO HELP MAKE ME A MORE PROACTIVE VOLLEYER?

A: Here's a great one: Visualize a cone angling out about 45 degrees from your mouth—just like a giant, super wide megaphone.

THE VIEW FROM ABOVE:

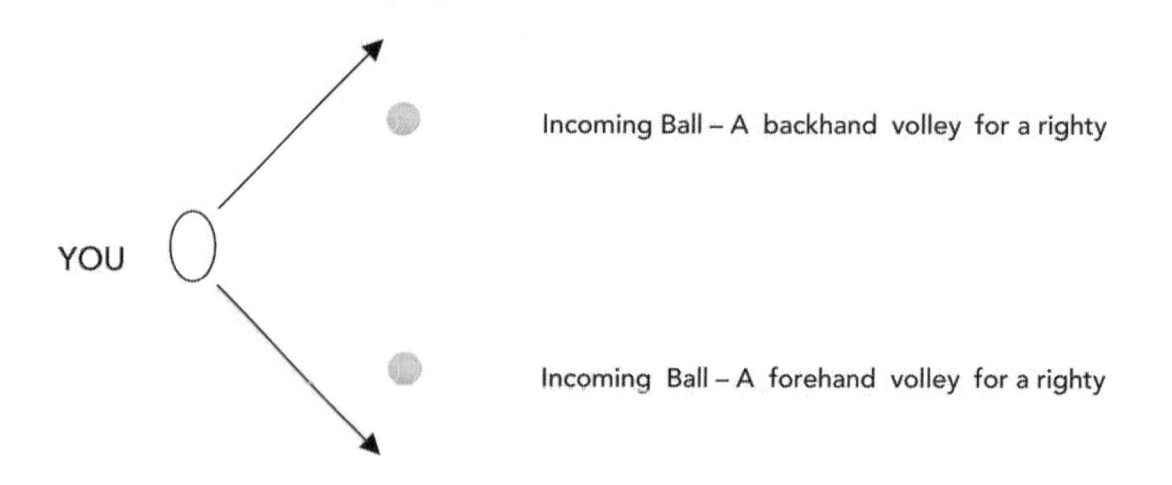

YOU

Incoming Ball – A backhand volley for a righty

Incoming Ball – A forehand volley for a righty

Now, let's use that megaphone to improve your volley game.

- All you have to do is keep your contact point within the side angles of the megaphone! As long as you do that, you'll preempt a slew of potential problems commonly associated with late contact.

If you utilize this visualization consistently for even an hour, you'll see dramatic improvements not only in your volleys—of which early contact is a key component—but in your mental attitude as well. You'll stay doubly sharp, because your focus on early contact not only *requires* a proactive state of mind—it also *sustains* that proactive state of mind!

So grab your megaphone and start spreading the news: "Watch out, my friend—there's a lean, mean volleying machine on this side of the net!"

THE "ZORRO" TRICK

Q: I'M GETTING KILLED IN RAPID EXCHANGES AT THE NET. WHAT'S THE BEST WAY TO HANDLE QUICK, CONSECUTIVE VOLLEYS?

A: Rapid exchanges at the net are a lot like fencing, full of thrusts and counter-thrusts. So play it smart and emulate the master swordsman Zorro.

- Whenever possible, recover to an *en garde* position after each volley!

When you're en garde for a volley:

- Your racket hand is directly in front of you, with the tip of your racket angled up about 45 degrees.
- Your non-dominant hand is supporting your racket at the throat.

What's the benefit of being en garde? Well, there's an old fencing joke that goes something like this:

- "What do you call a lazy fencer who lets their sword drift or dangle?"

The answer, of course, is "Dead!"—and that point is equally well taken for a tennis player at the net. If you let your racket drift or dangle, you're simply inviting disaster.

So stay alert and en garde to parry your opponent's rapier thrusts. Fortunately, you won't really have to face a sharp point at the net—but if you recover to en garde after every volley, you'll often have the opportunity to win one!

8

SPECIALTY SHOT MAGIC

QUESTIONS	TRICKS	
I have a *lot* of trouble with low forehand volleys. What's the fix?	*Grip 1 – Forehand Volley*	151
How can I hit that spectacular crosscourt counter-drop I've seen on TV? You know— the one that practically travels from sideline to sideline.	*Grip 2 – Forehand Volley Extreme*	152
I get so tense on easy overheads that I either blow it, or I can't quite put them away. I could just cry!	*Rib*	153
I try some touch shots, but I never have much luck with them. Can I develop feel, or do I just have to be born with it?	*Kissing*	155

Sometimes I hit a pretty fair drop shot—but I hit some real clunkers too! What's a sure-fire way to improve my consistency?	*Hawk*	156
My underspin game is kind of spotty—especially when it comes to directing my approach shots. How can I tighten it up?	*Flashlight*	157
Even some short lobs are going over my head. How can I get back under them in time to hit an overhead smash?	*Cell Phone*	158

THE "GRIP" TRICK 1 – FOREHAND VOLLEY

Q: I HAVE A *LOT* OF TROUBLE WITH LOW FOREHAND VOLLEYS. WHAT'S THE FIX?

A: When you have time to do so, tweak your grip a little toward backhand grip. That small shift will give you extra net clearance, and save you from having to play a potentially weak shovel shot.

Start with your racket in your normal forehand volley grip—*hopefully, Continental, as in the photo below*—and play a few forehand volleys.

Then, use your non-dominant hand to rotate the racket ever so slightly toward backhand grip (clockwise for a right-hander, counterclockwise for a lefty).

- Now, as you prepare to volley, the top (three o'clock) edge will be slightly further away from the net than it was in Continental grip, and the bottom (nine o'clock) edge will be correspondingly closer.

Bottom Edge Of The Racket

It's important to remember to always *open your hitting hand* before you adjust your grip with your non-dominant hand. Otherwise, *you'll only rotate your entire hand/racket unit*—rather than actually changing the position of the grip within your hitting hand as intended.

Now, hit another forehand volley, moving your strings straight forward through the ball.

- If the bottom edge of your racket is leading as it should be, then just like magic you'll see the ball leave your strings in a nice upward arc, with beautiful backward rotation as well.

The more you tweak your grip toward Eastern backhand, the more arc you'll automatically obtain—and the shorter your shot will land in the court. So this trick is golden for drop shots and counter drops when you're close to the net.

Grip Trick 1 is a great marriage of biomechanics and physics that you definitely want to add to your repertoire. When you use it, you'll never again have to *try* to add some underspin to your shot, because it'll be there all by itself. And just as importantly, this tweak guarantees some extra net clearance—which is vital to your success in making those tough low volleys!

THE "GRIP" TRICK 2 – FOREHAND VOLLEY EXTREME!

Q: HOW CAN I HIT THAT SPECTACULAR CROSSCOURT COUNTER-DROP I'VE SEEN ON TV? YOU KNOW—THE ONE THAT PRACTICALLY TRAVELS FROM SIDELINE TO SIDELINE.

A: That's a job for Grip Trick Extreme—the bigger, badder version of Grip Trick 1 on the preceding page. This variation is an easy tweak that will give you good net clearance and help you find that sharp angle as well.

- In Grip Trick 1 you learned to rotate your racket slightly toward backhand grip to get extra loft and underspin on your forehand volleys. In this Extreme version, you'll rotate it a smidge further with your non-dominant hand: Clockwise if you're a right-hander—counterclockwise if you're a lefty.

    Rotate the frame until *the base knuckle of the index finger of your hitting hand* is resting on the top bevel of the grip. (That bevel is an extension of the top edge of the racket. See the diagrams in Chapter 2, pp. 15-16.)

Recognize that grip? It's Eastern backhand—and you're going to use it to play stunning crosscourt forehand angles!

- Here's a visual cue: When you look down at the *forehand* side of your strings in that grip, it should almost appear as if you're looking into a mirror or a frying pan. It's not *quite* that extreme—but almost!

The *downside* to using that grip to hit a forehand is that it's almost impossible to go *anywhere except crosscourt*. Now, that's a pretty significant negative—but in this case, it's going to work *for you* rather than against you.

- That combination of wrist bias and an extremely open racket face is a real winner when you need to hit a real winner. Nice, early contact is all it takes to send the ball up and over the net—and best of all, sharply crosscourt.

So amaze your friends with this most pro-ish of shots—and show off like the ham you know you are! This extreme version of Grip Trick 1 is sure to make you an artist around the net. So whenever the opportunity is there, go for it—and dazzle the gallery with your crosscourt masterpiece!

THE "RIB" TRICK

Q: I GET SO TENSE ON EASY OVERHEADS THAT I EITHER BLOW IT, OR I CAN'T QUITE PUT THEM AWAY. I COULD JUST CRY!

A: That's a tearful situation indeed! So let's begin with a brief review of the basic preparation for hitting an overhead.

1. Unless your opponent's lob is short, you'll almost always need to move away from the net, back toward the baseline. So start by taking a strong backward step with the foot under your hitting arm; that's the quickest way to rotate your trunk into a powerful hitting position. Then, stay sidewise to the net and use cross steps as necessary to move back under the ball.

2. Target the ball by pointing at it with the index finger of your non-dominant arm. Reaching up high with that hand will keep your front shoulder higher than your hitting shoulder, and position you for an efficient transfer of energy up into the shot.

3. Finally, avoid the pitfalls of a weak wrist position by keeping the tip of your racket pointing up toward the ball as you move under it. That will prevent you from

flopping your wrist back with your racket dangling behind you. That flopped back position is so mechanically weak it makes it tough *not* to hit a sloppy shot.

Congratulations: You've completed your preparation! Now it's just a matter of maintaining a relaxed hitting shoulder until the ball comes down. That's huge—because the last thing you want when you're ready to hit an overhead is tight, bunched up shoulder muscles.

To experience what that feels like, simply reach for the ceiling with your hitting hand and then grab the top of that shoulder with your other hand. See what I mean? Waiting like that does nothing to help you, and you still have to drop that shoulder before you can hit a smooth, powerful overhead.

That's where the "Rib" trick comes in:

- When you drop your hitting elbow you guarantee that your hitting shoulder will stay nice and relaxed. So as you wait for the ball to descend, keep that elbow below your shoulder, anywhere from 12 to 15 inches from your rib cage. That way it can't possibly creep up high enough to make your shoulder muscles tight.

Then, just relax with your hitting elbow pointed at the ground until you're good and ready to smash the ball and make your opponent sorry they ever dared to lob. As long as you remember to *Rib It,* cryin' time is over—and you'll never again have to endure any ribbing about a suspect overhead!

THE "KISSING" TRICK

Q: I TRY SOME TOUCH SHOTS, BUT I NEVER HAVE MUCH LUCK WITH THEM. CAN I DEVELOP FEEL, OR DO I JUST HAVE TO BE BORN WITH IT?

A: Anyone can improve their feel if they think of a touch shot as a kissing occasion. It's a perfect time to just kiss the ball with your strings.

Strings to the ball—that's what it's all about when you get down to the basic physics. *Hopefully,* your strings are your only point of contact with the ball—so a lot depends on how long that contact lasts.

Although it might seem logical that briefer contact will produce a more delicate shot, the reality is that *less contact means less control.* What you really need for maximum control is more contact—and you'll never get that if you poke or jab at the ball.

So use this fun visualization to help develop better feel:

- Every time you play a touch shot, pretend you're kissing the ball with your strings!

Now remember, one of the key elements of an outstanding kiss is *duration.* Try the following, and see if you agree:

- Close your eyes for a second and imagine you're kissing someone you think is absolutely adorable. Now tell me: Was it over in the blink of an eye, or did you try to make it last as looooong as you possibly could? If you did, it was probably pretty nice!

Duration is what made that kiss extra special—and it will do the same thing for your touch game. The longer the contact lasts the better your accuracy and consistency will be, so just relax and enjoy.

In general, I'm a huge fan of "Less is more"—but this is definitely a case where "More is more!" And you don't have to just limit your kissing to touch shots; extended contact will enhance every shot in your repertoire. So kiss and kiss as much as you want to, and make that contact last! Just kiss the ball with your strings—and fall in love with the game all over again!

THE "HAWK" TRICK

Q: SOMETIMES I HIT A PRETTY FAIR DROP SHOT—BUT I HIT SOME REAL CLUNKERS TOO! WHAT'S A SURE-FIRE WAY TO IMPROVE MY CONSISTENCY?

A: Watch the ball like a hawk! What a concept: I'm amazed nobody's thought of it before. But seriously—it's always a great idea, and the trickier the shot, the more important it is to do that.

Once you decide to play a drop shot, it's impossible to watch the ball too closely!

- So lock onto it like a diving peregrine falcon, and watch the seams as they spin. Forget about sneaking a peek at your opponent—just execute the shot as well as you possibly can.

Then, after you finish the action completely, you can turn your attention toward doing whatever needs to be done next.

Think of it this way:

- How carefully would you watch the ball if you were guaranteed a million dollar prize for being able to correctly identify the number printed on it?

That's the kind of visual concentration we're talking about here. And even if your only reward is a fantastic touch shot and a stunned look on your hapless opponent's face, that's still a pretty sweet deal.

What's more, consider this: If you use the "Hawk" trick at the right time at the right tournament, who's to say you *won't* win close to a million dollars? Just ask a French Open champion—they'll tell you all about it!

THE "FLASHLIGHT" TRICK

Q: MY UNDERSPIN GAME IS KIND OF SPOTTY—ESPECIALLY WHEN IT COMES TO DIRECTING MY APPROACH SHOTS. HOW CAN I TIGHTEN IT UP?

A: Light your path to success with a flashlight beam!

Underspin—affectionately known as the knife—is a vital component of a well-rounded game.

- It's a great neutralizer against an opponent who likes incoming pace and/or a nice high bounce, because you can use it to give them less of either.
- It can also be an excellent choice when you want to come to the net. A low bouncing approach shot will force your opponent to hit uphill to clear the net—and that increases your chances of getting an attackable volley.

So if lack of accuracy is all that's holding you back from fully utilizing your underspin game, this trick will definitely shed some light on the subject.

- What you're going to do is imagine there's a flashlight beam shining right out from the center of your strings—and then use that beam to illuminate the path you want the ball to follow!

Now in order to *keep* the path illuminated, you'll need to keep your strings moving right through the point of contact and out toward your target.

Here's your checklist:

1. Just before you touch the ball, shine the beam of light from the center of your strings out in the direction you want the ball to travel. If you're using an open, beveled racket face, the beam will obviously be shining at an upward angle. But that's a non-issue—all you're concerned with here is that the *forward* direction is on-line with your target.
2. Then, keep your flashlight beam shining in that direction as you move your strings through the point of contact.
3. Finally, continue shining the beam forward even after the ball has left your strings. That way, the ball can see the exact path you want it to follow!

If you apply those steps you'll certainly garner a big improvement in accuracy. So shine your flashlight beam *before, during and after contact*—and start blinding your opponents with the brilliance of your underspin shots!

THE "CELL PHONE" TRICK

Q: EVEN SOME SHORT LOBS ARE GOING OVER MY HEAD. HOW CAN I GET BACK UNDER THEM IN TIME TO HIT AN OVERHEAD SMASH?

A: The secret is a Quick Initial Reaction—code acronym: QIR. By quick, I mean the *instant* the lob leaves your opponent's strings!

Unless it's a real shortie, you need to immediately turn your body at least 90 degrees toward your forehand side—and then move under the lob as quickly as you can. Efficient striking mechanics are an asset, but won't help a bit if you can't touch the ball.

Here's a great way to develop that quick initial reaction:

- Pretend you're expecting a call on your cell phone—*and that if you can answer it within the first three rings, you'll win the set outright!*

Sounds pretty easy, huh? But there's one little catch: Your cell phone is on the ground next to the back fence, and you have no idea when the call is coming. Now think how quickly you'd turn and run when you heard that first ring: Greased lightening—if not faster.

That's just how quickly you need to turn—or at least rotate—for almost any lob. Turn instantly, and then start moving to position yourself under the ball. True, you might not gain outright victory with one smash—but you'll sure feel like a winner when you get back under the ball in time for a great overhead!

PART IV

MAXIMIZE YOUR PHYSICAL CAPABILITIES

9
BODY MAGIC

QUESTIONS

Pros always seem so on balance, but I feel like a klutz half the time. What am I missing—and don't say, "Way too many shots!"

When is it critical that I *not* worry too much about getting ready for my next shot?

I don't seem to be able to get to some shots that aren't all that far away. How can I cover more of them?

I've heard about using weight transfer to add more power to my shots. How do I go about it?

I'm so tense my muscles have stopped working right. How can I loosen up?

TRICKS

Conquistador – Part 1	165
Conquistador – Part 2	166
Collapse It	167
Nose To The Ball: Groundies & Volleys	168
Jog It Out	169

I hit some great shots—but I hit some real stinkers too! How can I improve my consistency?	Hold That Pose	170
Sometimes I get so nervous I can't even breathe! How can I regroup?	Breathe Easy	171
One minute I'm moving great—and then suddenly I'm a slug! Is there a trick to help keep my feet moving?	As Above, So Below	173
I'm habitually late with my contact—and it gets worse under pressure. How can I kick-start myself?	Drill Sergeant	174
Why do pros almost always take a practice swing after a missed shot—and why should I do the same thing?	Model It	175
I feel really unstable on a lot of my shots. Exactly what does it mean to be *grounded*, and how will that help me play better?	Squashing Grapes	176
Sometimes my racket twists in my hand at the moment of impact. How can I remedy that?	Squeeze	177
I've got a good quick first step, but I still get passed way too often. What's wrong?	Sticky Foot	178

THE "CONQUISTADOR" TRICK – Part 1

Q: PROS ALWAYS SEEM SO ON BALANCE, BUT I FEEL LIKE A KLUTZ HALF THE TIME. WHAT AM I MISSING—AND DON'T SAY, "WAY TOO MANY SHOTS!"

A: The best way to resolve your balance issues is to claim the area around the ball as your very own. Think of it as a Conquistador thing.

Five hundred years ago in the bad old days of rampant imperialism, Conquistadors would wade ashore, plant their flag, and brazenly proclaim, "I claim this land for Spain!" Easy for them to say—but quite a surprise to the locals, no doubt!

The Conquistadors were right about one thing, however: *Possession of* and *declaration of* are powerful concepts—and they're perfect antidotes for chronic klutz syndrome.

Here's how to apply those principles on court:

- Whenever possible, declare possession of the area around the ball—before, during, and sometimes *even after* contact!

Whether you prefer to hit with your feet planted firmly on the ground or leap aggressively into your shots, you gain a distinct advantage when you establish your balance just prior to your final action. You can accomplish that in three easy steps:

1. Stake your claim to the ideal hitting location by getting there as quickly as possible.
2. Once you're there, load up your strong leg (the one supporting your weight at contact) and really dig those toes into the court.
3. Finally—whether you choose to crouch, stand or leap—reinforce your claim by being fully present. In other words, control that location with your body, mind and spirit until you've *fully completed* your best possible effort.

From the very first time you incorporate these principles, your sense of what it feels like to be well balanced during play will change forever. To know that feeling is to love it, and the key to owning it is simple:

- Always strive for complete command of that one moment in time and place—the meeting between you and the ball.

So grab your helmet and banner, Conquistador. Claim that moment for your very own, and banish your chronic klutz syndrome to the scrap heap of history!

THE "CONQUISTADOR" TRICK – Part 2

Q: WHEN IS IT CRITICAL THAT I *NOT* WORRY TOO MUCH ABOUT GETTING READY FOR MY NEXT SHOT?

A: Oddly, it's when you're in trouble because you've been pulled out wide. In that emergency situation, your best play is to stay *on location* for a fraction of a second after the ball leaves your strings!

Seldom is the difference between a club player and a pro more apparent than when they're pulled out wide. They both know they need to hit a good shot and then quickly recover to the undefended part of the court—*but there's a world of difference in their time management.*

The club player will start to run back to the open court *while* they're hitting their shot, abandoning the contact zone as quickly as they can. Wrong!

- The pro, on the other hand, invests a little more time at the point of contact—*in hope of hitting a better shot!*

Yes, you do need to get ready for your next shot; and yes, you may need to dash a long way to cover it. But your first priority is *to make an effective shot*—and that's tough to do while you're falling back toward the open court.

- A strong shot is always your first and best line of defense!

That's why pros consistently choose balance—with it's inherent potential for weight transfer and/or extended contact—over an early exit.

- Nine times out of ten, *a strong shot from a weak location is better than a weak shot with a quick getaway!*

So ignore the balance-killing urge to bail out while the ball is still on your strings. Stake your claim, Conquistador, and boldly claim that trouble spot—before, during and after contact. "Plan A" is always about balance and commitment—even when you're in trouble. That falling away stuff is strictly "Emergency Plan Z!"

THE "COLLAPSE IT" TRICK

Q: I DON'T SEEM TO BE ABLE TO GET TO SOME SHOTS THAT AREN'T ALL THAT FAR AWAY. HOW CAN I COVER MORE OF THEM?

A: Many coaches teach that the best way to move laterally is to push off with your opposite leg. In other words, in order to move left you push off with your right leg, and vice versa. But Tennis Magic is here to declare there's an even better way to get from point A to point B!

- In actuality, the quickest way to move forward *or* laterally is to collapse the leg closest to your intended destination, while you lean hard in that direction.

Remember when you were a kid, and somebody would sneak up behind you and push your knee forward? And remember how fast you would start to fall before you could catch yourself? That's a perfect example of this principle in action.

- Anytime you lean—while simultaneously collapsing your knee like that—the force of gravity jet-propels you in the direction you want to go.

But don't let the jet thing scare you. When you lean and collapse one leg, the other leg automatically crosses over to catch you, so there's no increased risk of falling. And best of all, there's no thinking involved—because you mastered this years ago!

As a toddler, you intuitively learned that if one leg starts to give out, all you have to do is catch yourself with the other one.

It may not have been pretty at first, but boy did you catch on fast—and before you could say Huggies you were lurching around to your little heart's content!

So fear not: If you're old enough to read, this one's a piece of cake. It requires no more athletic ability than whatever you're doing now—and the only thing that might take a little getting used to is your newfound ability to cover the court. Every time you lean and "Collapse It" you'll get a great jump on your opponent's shots—and that's a huge step toward getting *their* game to collapse!

THE "NOSE TO THE BALL" TRICK – GROUNDIES AND VOLLEYS

Q: I'VE HEARD ABOUT USING WEIGHT TRANSFER TO ADD MORE POWER TO MY SHOTS. HOW DO I GO ABOUT IT?

A: Try to touch the ball with the tip of your nose just before you start to bring your racket forward!

Incorporating a little weight transfer into your shots is a great way to get the extra power you're looking for. Here's how to add sting to both your groundies and volleys:

- Just before you strike the ball, move your *nose, head and shoulders* three or four inches toward it. Allow your upper body to follow your nose in a natural manner—in other words, don't just jut out your neck and face like you're doin' the Funky Chicken!

> Patrick Rafter, like most great volleyers, was superbly consistent in taking his nose, head and shoulders toward the ball for maximum proactive effect.

A small forward shift is more than enough to significantly increase the power and crispness of your shots, and three or four inches are all you need. It's easy and effective: So always take your nose to the ball—and let weight transfer power up your game!

THE "JOG IT OUT" TRICK

Q: I'M SO TENSE MY MUSCLES HAVE STOPPED WORKING RIGHT. HOW CAN I LOOSEN UP?

A: If you feel like you're starting to choke and your body is locking up on you, jog it out!

Jogging is a great way to counteract the dreaded *choke syndrome,* so start by jogging in place for ten seconds. Then, shift your weight onto the balls of your feet and swivel your hips from side to side a few times to loosen up your lower body.

Some days, that'll be all you need to do to get back on track—*but not always.* No matter how well you're moving from the waist down, your upper body can still start locking up on you—and when that happens it can be tough to finish your shots freely, if at all!

UPPER BODY ISSUES

To address upper lockup, first jog it out for a few seconds to (A) clear your mind and (B) keep yourself loose from the waist down. Then, incorporate a little modeling between points.

- Model a few brisk forehands, backhands, serves or volleys—whatever you feel is most appropriate. And as you model the shots, make sure you take your body and racket through the full range of motion. (See the "Model It" trick in this chapter.)

You'll find that a little modeling goes a long way toward breaking those waist-up choke chains—especially if you focus on smooth acceleration and an ideal finish after going through the full range of motion.

Let's face it: Tension is an inescapable element of competitive play, and sooner or later you're bound to experience some physical constrictions caused by stress. The good news is, you can minimize the impact by using the "Jog It Out" trick to offset the effects. So whether it's a waist down, waist up, or full body choke—remember to start your recovery by jogging it out. It's a superb antidote for that kind of tension!

THE "HOLD THAT POSE" TRICK

Q: I HIT SOME GREAT SHOTS—BUT I HIT SOME REAL STINKERS TOO! HOW CAN I IMPROVE MY CONSISTENCY?

A: When you start your warm up—or during a ball machine or drill session—get on track right away by holding the finish of each and every shot for a count of two after contact.

When you hold your pose exactly as you would during a photo shoot, you'll gain a really clear sense of what just happened.

- Then, anything that needs adjusting—whether balance, preparation, or a technical issue—will be much easier to identify and correct.

Start your assessment by asking, "How is my balance?" If it seems shaky, address your distance from the ball as a possible cause. Some of the usual suspects in that regard are:

- Late racket and/or body preparation for the specific shot you have in mind.
- A late start moving toward the ideal hitting location.
- Misjudging the speed or the direction of the ball.
- Misjudging the depth or *lack of depth* of the ball.
- Misjudging the spin. Spin dramatically affects both the height and trajectory of the ball *after* the bounce.

Any small miscalculation in distance can wreak havoc with your shot making, so pay close attention in that area before you move on to the final step.

I'M READY FOR MY CLOSE UP, MR. DeMILLE . . .

Remember: *Whatever you did last is what you're most likely to do next!* So the final step is to triple-check your finish for anything that's uncomfortable or technically inefficient.

- If you do find something that needs tweaking, carefully and deliberately adjust the ending of your stroke.
  - *Then, hold that adjusted pose for a full two seconds!*

When you maintain that picture perfect hold, you embed the correction at an auto-respond core level—which is exactly where it should reside. So plant the seeds of consistency early in order to weed out those stinkers that are plaguing you. Hold that pose during drills and warm-up—and clean up your finish right at the start!

THE "BREATHE EASY" TRICK

Q: SOMETIMES I GET SO NERVOUS I CAN'T EVEN BREATHE! HOW CAN I REGROUP?

A: Quick . . . use this secret breathing trick while there's still time!

There are two very different causes that can make you feel that way:

1. Shortness of breath is usually the first sign that you've been pushed toward your physical limit. It doesn't necessarily indicate that you're out of shape; even the most well conditioned athlete might need to suck wind after a tough point.

2. A more insidious possibility is that *nerves are kicking your butt!* Nervous tension can be even *more* debilitating than a long, grueling point.

Marat Safin can tell you all about it. At the 2000 US Open—with match point in hand—he was all set to serve to Pete Sampras when he accidentally dropped a ball. Later, in a TV interview, he said that at that moment he was so affected by nerves he wasn't sure he could even bend over to pick it up! Luckily, a ball boy darted out before his dilemma was exposed, and Marat collected himself enough to serve. It was a good one, and he won his first Grand Slam tournament when Pete netted the return.

Now, none of us will ever be in that exact predicament—but you can certainly expect to face similar stresses against opponents of your own skill level. And whether it's fatigue or nerves that are affecting you, this trick can be a real lifesaver when your heart is pounding and you feel like you're suffocating.

In that situation you'll have only about thirty seconds to pull yourself together—and your response can spell the difference between victory and defeat. But no worries; your road to recovery is only four steps long!

THE BREATHE EASY STEPS

Step 1: First, put down your racket and stand up nice and straight. Then, raise your arms high overhead and press your palms together as you breathe in through your nose.

Step 2: Exhale *slowly* through your mouth while slowly bending forward as far as you can. By the time you finish, with your hands dangling by your ankles, you should have squeezed every drop of air out of your lungs.

Step 3: Start your return to an upright position. As you rise, slowly lift your arms and begin to inhale. Keep your inhalation even and continuous, and fill your lungs *from bottom to top* in the following sequence:

- First, fill your *abdomen* as you raise your arms to that level. But inhale slowly—because you're only a third of the way home!

- Then, fill the area *at heart level* as you continue to raise your arms.

- Finally, fill the *top third of your lungs with as much air as they can hold*—and finish with your arms extended high up over your head and your body completely erect.

Step 4: Perfect! Now you're ready to send every last bit of that oxygen to your brain by pressing your palms together over your head as hard as you can. Then, *press even harder as you silently count to ten!* Finally, release and exhale.

Ahhhhhhhhhh . . . back to life, and none the worse for wear!

Now, don't worry if you feel a little woozy or lightheaded for several seconds after you finish. That's just your brain's initial response to the massive influx of oxygen you've given it. Once that wave washes by, you'll feel revitalized, calm and relaxed—and well you should. The crisis has passed, and you're ready and able to re-enter the fray. You've taken a wonderful thirty-second vacation—and now you can breathe easy once again!

THE "AS ABOVE, SO BELOW" TRICK

Q: ONE MINUTE I'M MOVING GREAT—AND THEN SUDDENLY I'M A SLUG! IS THERE A TRICK TO HELP KEEP MY FEET MOVING?

A: This trick will get you on track from the waist down by getting you on track from the waist up!

There are various reasons why—without any warning at all—your preparation and footwork can suddenly vanish. It could be nerves, fatigue or even "X, the Unknown." But whatever the reason, watch out! Unless you nip it right in the bud, your entire game could be in imminent danger of going right down the tubes.

You might be familiar with the time-honored 20th century technique of saying to yourself, "Move your feet"—and if that solves your problem, then all's well and good. But if you think you need a slightly stronger tonic, here's an even more effective method for achieving the results you want.

- Speak the word "Ready!" Say it aloud to yourself the exact second the ball either (A) lands in your opponent's court, or (B) touches their strings—whichever comes first.

In that context, "Ready" functions as both a command *and* an affirmation—and verbalizing it releases a powerful tonic that mobilizes you into action.

Now I certainly don't mean to disrespect our dear old friend "Move your feet"—especially after such long and noble service! But everybody deserves a rest sooner or later. So why not start kickin' it 21st century style? Kick-start your feet by kick-starting your mind with the conscious *action command* "Ready!" Remember: "As above, so below. Free your mind, and your feet will go!"

THE "DRILL SERGEANT" TRICK

Q: I'M HABITUALLY LATE WITH MY CONTACT—AND IT GETS WORSE UNDER PRESSURE. HOW CAN I KICK-START MYSELF?

A: Make a commitment to turn your shoulders the second you see the ball leave your opponent's strings. That's a great kick-starter to get you going.

The mystery of why we sometimes freeze under pressure is buried deep within the mind-body connection. Nerves and emotions are powerful forces—and when you add a little stress to the mix, the relay wire from your brain to your feet can start sparking like a Roman candle. Suddenly you're in a Fellini movie—and the bad news is, you're the clown!

Players have described it by saying, "I felt paralyzed," or, "I felt like I was glued to the court." Luckily, there's a Tennis Magic Drill Sergeant on call who will be happy to make sure that that never happens to you.

- Imagine you have the letter *L* sewn on the outside of your left shoulder, and the letter *R* on the outside of your right shoulder.

Got it? Now, as soon as the ball leaves your opponent's racket, you're going to hear the word "Turn!" ring out in your head. That's because Sarge is standing right behind you bellowing it at the top of his lungs—and boy, is he loud!

Here's how to keep him happy:

- Respond to that command by making a hard *hip and shoulder turn*—clockwise or counterclockwise as necessary. Rotate as quickly as you can, and make sure you turn far enough for him to see your appropriate shoulder patch from right where he's standing.

Great—*you've done something!* You're no longer a frozen statue of General About Toulouse, just before his famous surrender.

- With Sarge barking at you, you can't possibly fall victim to nervous paralysis—so listen up and jump lively! Your great quick-turn reflex will get you going, and once you've been kick-started you're much less likely to be late.

So use the "Drill Sergeant" trick whenever you sense that your overall level of proactivity is dipping, and lead-foot is setting in. Every time you turn on cue you'll make both Sarge and yourself proud—and he told me he has complete confidence in your ability to take it from there!

THE "MODEL IT" TRICK

Q: WHY DO PROS ALMOST ALWAYS TAKE A PRACTICE SWING AFTER A MISSED SHOT—AND WHY SHOULD I DO THE SAME THING?

A: We do that to clear our body's *muscle memory* of the residual effects of any flaw that might have crept into our stroke pattern. *You* should do it because it works!

The process is called modeling: The purpose is to overwrite the muscle memory associated with an error and replace it with a *new and improved memory pattern.*

- Once you model a correction you'll be much more likely to succeed on your next attempt, because your body will use that new, more efficient pattern in lieu of the previous one. It's a simple biomechanical fact that:
  - "Whatever you did last is what you're most likely to do next!"

So always reformat your hard drive after a missed shot by taking your body and racket through a full, corrected range of motion—all the way from start to finish. It's a powerful tool, and you don't have to be Maria Sharapova or Serena Williams to reap the benefit of big time modeling. It's available to everyone—and if you do it enough, who knows: That just might be *you* modeling on next month's cover of "Tennis" magazine!

THE "SQUASHING GRAPES" TRICK

Q: I FEEL REALLY UNSTABLE ON A LOT OF MY SHOTS. EXACTLY WHAT DOES IT MEAN TO BE "GROUNDED," AND HOW WILL THAT HELP ME PLAY BETTER?

A: If you feel unstable even when you're not under duress, chances are you've lost connection with the ground. The cure is to really grab the court with your toes and the balls of your feet.

A fun way to learn that feeling is to pretend you're making wine the old fashioned way. Before the days of mechanical presses, villagers used their feet to squash the annual grape harvest. I bet that was quite a party—especially if they had some of last year's wine left over! But here, we'll just settle for the intoxication of playing great, balanced tennis.

- Imagine you're standing in a tub full of beautiful, luscious grapes. First, lift both your heels slightly and shift your weight onto the balls of your feet. Then, squash some grapes by slowly pivoting your heels from side to side.

That's what it feels like to be consciously connected to the ground! And once you shift your weight onto the balls of your feet, you'll be ready to spring into action and do whatever needs to be done next.

Obviously, this is a great trick to use whenever you need to reestablish your *physical* equilibrium—but it has an even wider application. It's also great for restoring your *mental* and/or *emotional* equilibrium.

- When you establish a conscious connection with the court by squashing grapes, it *grounds* you in the broadest sense of the word, and produces a positive effect in all three of those areas.

So apply this trick across the board, and don't limit it to groundies. If you're serving and don't feel grounded, squash some grapes before you serve. If you're receiving, make it the first part of your preparation as you take up your stance. Whatever the situation, "Squashing Grapes" is ideal for grounding yourself physically, mentally and emotionally. Once you do that, you'll feel better and you'll play better—which all in all is a mahvelous feeling!

THE "SQUEEZE" TRICK

Q: SOMETIMES MY RACKET TWISTS IN MY HAND AT THE MOMENT OF IMPACT. HOW CAN I REMEDY THAT?

A: An off-center hit is the most likely culprit. The good news is that whatever the cause, there's a simple biomechanical fix you can use to minimize twisting.

- All you need to do is squeeze your *bottom three fingers* right before impact! Squeezing locks the tendons in your wrist and really firms up the racket in your hand.

Tennis is a game of emergencies, and when the action starts to heat up no amount of hand-eye coordination will prevent the occasional mishit. It's a given that you won't always be able to find the sweet spot—so make it a habit to squeeze your bottom three fingers just prior to contact for maximum crispness and control.

- This body trick applies to all strokes *except serves and overheads,* for which a nice loose wrist is a valuable asset. So on those two shots, be sure you do *not* squeeze tightly with your ring finger and pinky.

But for crisp volleys and groundies, a firm grip rules—and once you eradicate the wobble factor by squeezing, your results will improve immediately. What's more, there's one additional bonus to be enjoyed:

- It's a lot easier to zoom in on specific corrections you might need to apply if there's no wobbly racket stuff clouding the issue.

So squeeze for success: It's a firm foundation from which to apply your various Tennis Magic tricks. A firm wrist makes for solid shot making—and that's an essential element of a solid game!

THE "STICKY FOOT" TRICK

Q: I'VE GOT A GOOD QUICK FIRST STEP, BUT I STILL GET PASSED WAY TOO OFTEN. WHAT'S WRONG?

A: If you're having trouble cutting off volleys that aren't all that far away from you, it's probably because you're taking that quick first step with the wrong foot!

What I mean is, you're probably stepping out with the foot that's closest to the ball (bad idea!) rather than leaning and collapsing toward it like you should. (See the "Collapse It" trick in this chapter: It's a vital concept!)

- When you need to cut off a *wide volley,* never start by stepping out toward it with the foot that's closest to the ball. Starting that way drastically limits your range!
    - So if it's wide left, *never* start by stepping out toward it with your left foot. And if it's wide right, *never* start with your right foot.

That's because the further you step out with that foot, the more of an obstruction that foot becomes. In order to keep going, you then have to hoist your other leg over that foot—because it's totally pinned under your body weight once you step out wide.

So let's give you a "Sticky Foot" that'll make things easy—no matter how new this is to you or how ingrained your old habits might be.

- Just pretend your foot on the side you want to move toward is *glued to the court* for a fraction of a second after the ball leaves your opponent's strings!
    - That's your "Sticky Foot"—and because it's glued for a fraction of a second, you have no choice but to collapse that leg and lean hard toward the ball.

That hard lean will definitely get you off to a rocket start, and the advantage is a telling one. It'll help you say "Goodbye" to getting passed way too often—and "Hello" to passing your opponent in the score!

Part V

Your Greatest Asset: Your Mind

10
MENTAL EDGE MAGIC

QUESTIONS	TRICKS	
Sometimes I'm pretty timid out there. Can you help me be more aggressive?	*Cat*	187
Sometimes everything seems to be happening so fast. How can I keep my mind centered and calm?	*Make The World Stop Spinning*	188
I'm off to the worst start of my life. Help me before I kill again!	*You Cannot Be Serious!*	189
I know momentum is a big factor in sports. How can I tune in to the ebb and flow so I can ride those waves to victory?	*Surfer*	190

What should I do when everything's going against me? I feel like giving up and going home!	*Graph – It's Only A Blip!*	191
What's the single most important thing I can do to maintain a positive mental attitude on court?	*Fork In The Road*	192
If they come to the net on me one more time I'm gonna scream! How can I cope with that constant pressure?	*Now I've Got You*	193
My opponent seems to get every single lucky break. Am I just destined to lose?	*Do It Anyway*	194
I miss *way* too many easy put-aways—and it seems like the more I want it, the worse I do. What's going wrong?	*Zen Reverse-Mind*	195
What should I do 100 percent of the time after I make a great get?	*Reward And Punishment 1*	196
What should I always do after my opponent fails to finish off an easy put-away?	*Reward And Punishment 2*	196
How can I maintain my concentration when it starts to drift?	*Millionaire*	197
Yikes! I'm playing the number 1 seed in the next round, and I'm not that good. Do I have any real chance?	*Desire*	198

Every little noise out here is driving me crazy. Help me quick, or I'm gonna go ballistic!	Roar Of The Crowd	199
How can anybody be so lucky? And I'm not just talking about once or twice—it's every other doggone shot!	Understanding Luck	200
Sometimes I panic during a tough point. What's the secret to staying cool under pressure?	Air Conditioner	201
Surprises surprise me! How can I handle them better?	Be Prepared	202
I let way too many balls go by me at the net in doubles—and by the time I decide to act it's too late. How can I get my motor going up there?	Cobra	203
I sometimes tighten up and react more slowly as play starts to speed up. OK . . . I've even been known to freeze up once or twice! Can you quick thaw me?	Do It Now	204
Once I start missing a shot, it's all over! How can I nip that in the bud?	Eraser – Part 1	205
How can I get the most out of modeling?	Eraser – Part 2	206
How can I take better advantage of my opportunities after I hit a good shot?	Eye See You	207

My opponent is pretty doggone clever, and I'm tired of getting fooled out there. What's my best countermeasure?	*I Knew You Were Going To Do That*	208
Which is more important—my offense or my defense?	*Indy 500*	209
How can I keep from getting down on myself after I miss an easy shot?	*Ideal Picture*	210
I can tell it's going to be one of those days. Please make it all go away!	*Pretend*	210
What can I do right from the start of a match to help maintain a relaxed state of mind?	*Prepare To Relax*	211
Sometimes I'm indecisive in my shot selection. Is there a trick for that too?	*Read My Lips*	212
I'm not much of a poacher in doubles, and sometimes I space out at the net. How can I stay alert so I'm ready when the ball *does* come to me?	*Ready Mind*	213
I often hit late, even when I'm ready in time. What I need is a trick to help me pull the trigger sooner.	*Strings To The Ball*	214
Sometimes caffeine seems to help me play awesome tennis—but other times it seems to really mess me up. Can I tame that tiger?	*Un-Jolt Me*	214

THE "CAT" TRICK

Q: SOMETIMES I'M PRETTY TIMID OUT THERE. CAN YOU HELP ME BE MORE AGGRESSIVE?

A: The truly aggressive player is the archetypal cat ready to pounce—and when you emulate that mindset, lots of good things start to unfold.

For the truly aggressive player there's only one object of desire, and that's the ball! There's no doubt in their mind that it belongs to them—so naturally they stay extraordinarily alert.

- They totally adopt the mind-set of a predator, and believe that as soon as the ball leaves their opponent's strings, it's theirs! Like any hunter, they won't be successful all the time—but they never let that deter them in either attitude or action.

Their intense desire keeps them alert, and that combination of desire and alertness is a powerful pairing. Take the phenomenon called *home field advantage*. It's not just a familiarity with physical surroundings—it's much more a function of the intense desire of the home team or player to please their fans. That driving urge often leads to extraordinarily high levels of performance, and has been directly responsible for countless astounding upsets.

So whether you're a baseliner, all-courter, or serve-volleyer, remember that *desire and alertness* are key elements of an aggressive game. After all, you can't possibly be timid when you're all pumped up to go after the ball. So if your goal is to be a more aggressive player, always maintain an alert, predatory attitude. Get catty and think pounce—then just prick up your ears and go get 'em!

THE "MAKE THE WORLD STOP SPINNING" TRICK

Q: SOMETIMES EVERYTHING SEEMS TO BE HAPPENING SO FAST. HOW CAN I KEEP MY MIND CENTERED AND CALM?

A: Calm your mind by taking an extra fraction of a second to completely finish each shot.

There's no doubt about it: The more pressure you're under, the more likely you are to feel as if the world is spinning out of control. So straighten your strings and take a little circle walk to calm down between points; then, use this trick to make the world stop spinning once the ball is back in play.

- As you play the next point, really focus on finishing each shot completely.
    - That's a great way to keep yourself in the moment and maintain your equilibrium under pressure—because in order to do that, you have to make a conscious decision to ignore the whirlwind around you.

Remember, no matter how crazy things get, you're still the captain of the ship of your mind. So take firm hold of the helm by investing the extra bit of concentration it takes to fully finish each shot.

If this seems like an unusual approach to calming the mind, consider this: In the classic Western, "Shane," a youngster who idolized the hero asked if the unique way he wore his pistol was the best way to wear it.

- After a moment's reflection Shane answered, "Well, it's as good as any—and better than most."

That elegant assessment applies equally well here. When everything's a blur and you need to make the world stop spinning, I'm confident you'll find this trick as good as any—and better than most.

THE "YOU CANNOT BE SERIOUS!" TRICK

Q: I'M OFF TO THE WORST START OF MY LIFE. HELP ME BEFORE I KILL AGAIN!

A: The best way to change that flow is to pick one specific isolated goal—and then focus on it to the exclusion of everything else.

Have you ever hit the courts on a beautiful day, and for no apparent reason gotten off to a horrendously bad start? I mean, a start so awful you felt like you'd never played tennis before in your life! That's enough to make you want to use one of John McEnroe's most notorious and enduring quotes. So go ahead and let it rip . . . "YOU CANNOT BE SERIOUS!"

Great! Now it's time to get back on track. Your first objective when everything's falling apart is to *regain your mental equilibrium*—and the best way to do that is to confine your focus initially to a single, narrow goal.

Below are some commands that will get you headed in the right direction—each of which starts with the word "just." That word emphasizes your commitment to isolate *one thing and one thing only.*

For forehands you might tell yourself:

- "Just use a smooth, relaxed loop," or (if you use a semi-western grip),
- "Just finish your topspin stroke over your non-dominant shoulder."

And for backhands you might say:

- "Just turn you body sooner" or,
- "Just go for full extension through the contact zone."

Now, although those are solid generic suggestions, it's best that you formulate your own pertinent, personal commands that (A) address the specific needs of the moment, and (B) harmonize with your individual playing style. Keep in mind that *short and sweet* rules here—because the tighter you set your focus, the sooner you'll escape from the dreaded "Awful Start" syndrome.

So if things are ugly early, first get the funk out of your system with your best Johnny Mc imitation. Ready? On three: "YOU CANNOT BE SERIOUS! Then, start your comeback from square one by focusing your attention on one simple, positive goal. That's a great first step—as well as a superb way to change a terrible start into a fantastic finish!

THE "SURFER" TRICK

Q: I KNOW MOMENTUM IS A BIG FACTOR IN SPORTS. HOW CAN I TUNE IN TO THE EBB AND FLOW SO I CAN RIDE THOSE WAVES TO VICTORY?

A: The key here is to take special note of any fluky or unlikely occurrences: They often herald a shift in momentum that can alter the course of an entire match.

Momentum is a lot like a fickle ocean current. One minute it can be right with you, taking you to warm tropical waters—and then ten minutes later you could be on your way to the South Pole! Fortunately—as unpredictable as momentum can be—you *can* learn to spot signs that a sea change is imminent.

- A major clue to watch out for is *anything that's way out of the norm.* If your shot hits the only twig out there and takes a crazy bounce, or your opponent misses an easy put-away into a wide open court, always take that as a sign that the tide has turned in your favor.

No matter how trivial it might seem at the moment, that lucky break could be the little swell that signals a major sea change in your favor. So take full advantage by making a strong declaration that the momentum has indeed shifted your way. Straighten your strings and say:

- "*That's* a good omen! *There it is—my little wave.* Now I'm going to ride that little wave all the way to the shore!"

When you declare that event to be your personal wave you activate the tremendous power of Fiat, which is "To make it so by speaking it." Once you do that, surfs up and looking good! So expect the best—and always be ready to ride your little wave all the way to the shore!

THE "GRAPH" TRICK – IT'S ONLY A BLIP!

Q: WHAT SHOULD I DO WHEN EVERYTHING'S GOING AGAINST ME? I FEEL LIKE GIVING UP AND GOING HOME!

A: The only thing that can trump a Murphy's Law day is PMA: Positive Mental Attitude.

According to Murphy's Law, "Anything that can possibly go wrong probably *will* go wrong." Now, we both know that's ridiculous . . . except on certain days when it's 100 percent true!

On a Murphy Day the wind will always gust up at the worst possible time, and the sun will always pop out from behind the clouds to blind you just as you're ready to hit your shot. Dogs will bark, cell phones will ring, birds will dive, and babies will cry. So expect all of that, and then some!

The good news is, there's an easy way to rise above it.

- At moments such as that, use this magic phrase to re-connect with your vast inner reserve of strength, patience and fortitude. Simply recite the following words with *full conviction:*

> It's only a blip on the graph . . .
> It's just another little blip on the graph . . .
>
> **AND IT DOESN'T MATTER—**
> *BECAUSE I'M GOING TO WIN ANYWAY!*

Once you make that affirmation you'll instantly feel a warm glow, and all your stress will begin to fade. Then, birds can fly and babies can cry, and every net cord can trickle over and fall on your side . . .

- But it won't even matter—*because you know you're going to win anyway!*

The "Graph" trick is a lifejacket you can always depend on when a Murphy Day whirlpool starts tugging you down. So swim on bravely and never give up—and remember that the reward is great: The sweetest victories are the ones you achieve when everything's going against you!

THE "FORK IN THE ROAD" TRICK

Q: WHAT'S THE SINGLE MOST IMPORTANT THING I CAN DO TO MAINTAIN A POSITIVE MENTAL ATTITUDE ON COURT?

A: A sure-fire way to stay positive in all circumstances is to unconditionally accept *everything* that happens on court.

- A positive mental attitude reflects a shining expectation of a brighter future—regardless of temporary setbacks. So avoid the temptation to respond to failures with excuses. There's a higher, brighter path ahead of you that leads to freedom and empowerment.

Let's say your opponent stabs your brilliant approach shot and throws up a short desperation lob. Now, you've more than earned the easy kill—but as you set up under it, all you can see is the sun. Nevertheless, you fire away fearlessly—and frame it right into the net! Just like that, your sitting duck has turned into a lump of coal. Sacre bleu! How could anybody possibly *be* so lucky! (See "Understanding Luck" in this chapter.)

"So far, so bad," right? But the good news is you've arrived at a critical fork in the road, and there's a wonderful opportunity available to you. You can easily take the well-worn path and use the sun as an excuse—but if you're brave enough to take the road less traveled, your journey is sure to be a rewarding one.

- The first step is simple. Unconditionally accept what just happened—and take full responsibility for the misfire. Say to yourself:
  - "I just wasn't sharp enough *yet* today to make that shot!"

The word *yet* is key: It powerfully affirms your belief that soon you *will* be sharp enough to make it! So when you come to your fork in the road, remember the choice is yours:

- You can either seek comfort by criticizing your opponent's shot selection or execution, or you can rise to the challenge before you. You can choose blame, or you can choose personal responsibility!

If it's the latter, you've made a wonderful choice: Then, just focus on a positive future, and be inspired by Robert Frost's lovely poem, "The Road Less Traveled":

> "Two roads diverged in a wood, and I,
> I took the one less traveled by,
> And that has made all the difference."

THE "NOW I'VE GOT YOU!" TRICK

Q: IF THEY COME TO THE NET ON ME ONE MORE TIME I'M GONNA SCREAM! HOW CAN I COPE WITH THAT CONSTANT PRESSURE?

A: Shift to a mode of thinking in which you're always the predator—and *never* the victim.

There's an ancient wisdom quote on suffering that says, "It's not necessary to change external reality—just change your *perception* of it." You're suffering because you feel like a victim—so change your perception of events!

- A counter-puncher who loves a target and enjoys hitting passing shots almost never feels like a victim. When their opponent comes to the net their first reaction is *anticipation* rather than panic. They rejoice in the feeling, "Now I've got you!"—and that attitude is fundamental to their success.

So instead of cringing when your opponent puts pressure on you, your new and improved response is going to be "Great! Bring it on!" And although that might not initially feel either natural or genuine, it's an easily acquired habit.

- All you have to do is remember the mantra, *"Now I've got you!"*

Say that to yourself with complete conviction whenever your opponent comes charging in—and as your attitude changes, you'll find that you're able to respond in a much calmer and productive way.

Once you replace fear with anticipation you might even start thinking, *"Come on in—the water's fine! Get back in here: I dare you!"* And as you achieve greater and greater success, you might even wish they would come in on every point, so you can continue making them pay for their impudent attacks.

So much for responding to *their* offensive pressure: Now, let's turn the table on them with the same mantra!

- That power of "Now I've got you!" will always bring out your most positive, mentally proactive tennis—which makes it equally powerful when *you're* the one who's attacking.

So whether you're on offense or defense, say it loud and proud: "There's only one predator out here, and that's me—and now I've got you!" So go get 'em, tiger—cause now you've got 'em!

THE "DO IT ANYWAY" TRICK

Q: MY OPPONENT SEEMS TO GET EVERY SINGLE LUCKY BREAK. AM I JUST DESTINED TO LOSE?

A: That's a resounding "No!" Well, according to Shakespeare, anyway . . .

> "*Men at some time are masters of their fates;*
> *The fault, dear Brutus, is not in our stars,*
> *But in ourselves . . .*
>
> ~ Julius Caesar - 1599 - Act I. - Scene 2

So I'm pretty sure you're not destined to lose—and even if you are, you're not going down without a fight!

A pattern like the one you've described can definitely challenge your mental toughness and ability to maintain a positive attitude—and the doubt and frustration you're feeling are just natural responses to somebody getting away with that kind of stuff.

So go ahead and give it one last "Grrrr!" to clear the slate. Then, use this soliloquy to avoid the slough of despair, where many a player is dragged down, down, down into the cold, cold ground. Whenever your faith starts to waver, repeat this slowly and with the utmost conviction while you straighten your strings:

No matter how lucky they were on that last point . . .
No matter how unlucky I was on that last point . . .
No matter how well they played that last point . . .
No matter how badly I played that last point . . .

I'M GOING TO HOLD—OR BREAK—OR WIN—ANYWAY!

That's the mantra you want to affirm when adversity starts to wear on your positive mental attitude. Remember—a negative thought is just a pesky bird darting across the sky of your clear and focused mind. Here it comes, there it goes: Hello, goodbye, see you later. Your opponent's ridiculous luck is just dust in the wind, and certainly won't last forever. So back to the match, master of your fate—and don't forget to have fun. Grrrr!

THE "ZEN REVERSE-MIND" TRICK

Q: I MISS WAY TOO MANY EASY PUT-AWAYS—AND IT SEEMS LIKE THE MORE I WANT IT, THE WORSE I DO. WHAT'S GOING WRONG?

A: You're struggling because your burning desire to end those points is creating muscle tension—and tense muscles work much less efficiently than relaxed ones.

First of all, don't feel like the Lone Ranger. Everybody struggles with this, and sometimes even a little extra pressure can trigger a total meltdown. If you don't believe me, just try getting your house keys in the lock while the Boogeyman is chasing you. Not so easy, my friend!

So here's a fun fix that works from the top down to get those tense muscles nice and relaxed. It's the old "Zen Reversarooni":

- Rather than stressing about finishing off a kill shot, pretend you're trying really, really hard to just keep the point going *without ending it!*

That change in perspective can work miracles:

- Once you eliminate the stress of desperately wanting to end the point, you'll notice *just how easily you could finish it off if you really wanted to.* Then, a "Reverse Murphy's Law" kicks in—and everything that *can* possibly go right *does* go right!

If you've ever hit with a novice player or someone with limited mobility, you already know what it feels like to relax and just keep a rally going—and that's exactly how relaxed you want to be in closing out a point against a skilled, tenacious opponent.

So enter our hero, "Zen Reverse-Mind Man." He's here to inspire you to shift into Reverse-Mind mode—in which you could *care less* if the point keeps right on going!

- When you're no longer desperate to end things, it's easy to gear down to 75 percent on easy put-aways—and you'll be amazed at how well you play when you're content to keep them scrambling till they turn a nice shade of green!

So just take your pick: Drop shot, angle, or power. The possibilities are delicious—ripe plums on a low limb—and when you're that relaxed, it's hard *not* to finish the point that very second.

But, aw—what the heck; I guess it's finally time to put them out of their misery. So CRACK-POW; go ahead and wax a winner! Now *that's* my idea of a good time. Join the fun and enjoy your newfound freedom—and remember: "It's all in your mind!"

THE REWARD AND PUNISHMENT TRICKS
Two Sides Of The Same Coin

1. THE "REWARD" TRICK – TREAT YOURSELF!

Q: WHAT SHOULD I DO 100 PERCENT OF THE TIME AFTER I MAKE A GREAT GET?

A: Reward yourself! If you run a mile to keep a point going, you deserve a reward just for getting there—and your opponent certainly has no intention of giving you one. So reward yourself by always hitting the ball over the net!

That's your commitment, so let nothing deter you: And if you do happen to net a shot, nip that foolishness in the bud with your best manic coach impression.

- Say to yourself, "What the heck are you doing? You could have stayed right where you were and lost that point! If you're going to run that far for a ball, at least hit it over the @#*!% net!"

Why so rough? It's because you know better and you deserve better. You already know you aren't cosmically ordained to be the first player in history to win a point by hitting the ball into the net. (See the "Prime Directive" in Key Concepts.)

That just ain't gonna happen—never has, never will!

- So play smart, and always reward yourself after a great get.

In that situation, think of each and every shot you hit over the net as a Lotto ticket that just might turn out to be a big winner!

2. THE "PUNISHMENT" TRICK – PUNISH THEM!

Q: WHAT SHOULD I ALWAYS DO AFTER MY OPPONENT FAILS TO FINISH OFF AN EASY PUT-AWAY?

A: Use the flip side of the "Reward" trick to punish them any time they miss a duck.

- When you get a second chance on a ball they should have put away, condemn them *at the very least* to the misery of having to hit another shot!

Long-term, those odds are definitely in your favor, no matter how strong their court position. Nobody's perfect, and sooner or later you will get an error out of them.

So get that freebie back over the net any way you can—and punish them that way every time they choke on a kill. Remember, players have won Grand Slam tournaments by making their opponent hit *just one more shot*—and although you might not win Wimbledon with this trick, it'll sure help you beat Courtney down at the park!

THE "MILLIONAIRE" TRICK – "IS THAT YOUR FINAL ANSWER?"

Q: HOW CAN I MAINTAIN MY CONCENTRATION WHEN IT STARTS TO DRIFT?

A: By answering "Yes" to two questions before the start of each point.

A popular TV quiz show called "Who Wants To Be A Millionaire" had a great little catch phrase. The host would always ask contestants if their response was indeed their *final answer.*

That question forced them to take full personal responsibility, because once they answered, "Yes," they could never say "I was caught off guard" or "I don't know *what* I was thinking!"

Taking that personal responsibility often prevented them from making mindless mistakes—and it'll do wonders for you if you have trouble staying focused.

- A great way to keep your concentration high is to ask yourself two questions during the break between points:
    1. "Am I fully committed to making nice early contact with the ball?"
    2. "Am I ready to execute what needs to be done in a calm and relaxed manner?"

If you're able to answer "Yes" to both questions, you'll know your concentration is high and your mental preparation is excellent. Then, you can confidently give your opponent your firm, "Final answer!"

THE "DESIRE" TRICK

Q: YIKES! I'M PLAYING THE NUMBER 1 SEED IN THE NEXT ROUND, AND I'M NOT THAT GOOD. DO I HAVE ANY REAL CHANCE?

A: Accept the reality of the situation, and then win anyway by wanting it more!

Let's talk reality: Eventually you're going to come up against a player who is better than you in every aspect of the game—and to make things worse, they might also be a better athlete. Faced with those odds, what should you do?

- First of all, don't panic. You may be David and your opponent may be Goliath, but we all know what happened when they met in the finals! There's always a chance you can win by just wanting it more. Let me give you a classic example:

In 1983, there was an amazing NCAA basketball championship game in which the University of Houston's "Phi Slamma Jamma" line-up was a huge favorite over the North Carolina State Wolfpack. In the underdog's locker room before the game, things were grim and grimmer, and it was obvious to coach Jimmy Valvano that his boys were feeling the heat. They knew that all the pre-game hype was accurate, and that their opponents were awesomely talented. So guess what Coach Valvano did . . .

Rather than use those few precious moments to give a ridiculous rah-rah speech, he took a radically different approach.

- He told his players that everything they had heard was spot-on—*and that they could never match Houston in man for man talent!*

As he spoke, he could see their spirit sink to absolute rock bottom. Then, he played one of the most brilliant cards in coaching history. He concluded by saying, in effect:

- "I'm not going to stand here and tell you that you're better than them, because you're not. *But you don't have to be better than them to win this game. You just have to be better than them for 40 minutes!*"

Well, I'm sure I don't have to tell you what happened. In one of the greatest upsets in NCAA history, David toppled Goliath *with one final basket as the buzzer sounded*—and all it took was a regular sized portion of talent served with a huge side order of desire. The hopeless underdogs first accepted the reality of the situation—and then they won anyway *by wanting it more!*

So remember, even when you're truly over-matched, a burning desire for victory can move mountains. Boris Becker's famous quote about winning a deciding set in a big tournament sums it up beautifully: He said, "It's not really about tennis. It's about who wants it more!"

THE "ROAR OF THE CROWD" TRICK

Q: EVERY LITTLE NOISE OUT HERE IS DRIVING ME CRAZY. HELP ME QUICK, OR I'M GONNA GO BALLISTIC!

A: Whatever you do, don't fight it. Instead, issue a Royal Decree to this effect: Every noise I hear is actually *a source of encouragement—and can't possibly bug me!*

Sooner or later we all get hit with some sort of unexpected aural assault. It might be a lawn mower, a trash truck, a helicopter passing overhead, a pesky jaybird, a leaf blower, a car alarm, etc., etc., etc. And while there's no way to keep it from happening, you *can* control your response.

First and foremost, don't wrestle mentally with whatever it is that's bugging you: If you do, you're just going to get pinned!

- The real solution is to transform that noise into something positive!
    - Think of what a wonderful source of inspiration it would be if that distraction was simply the sound of spectators cheering you on.

So why stress? That's not a garbage truck working a dumpster: It's actually the sound of 5,000 people cheering for you at the top of their lungs!

Obviously, encouragement like that can't help but help—and you'll definitely gain an edge against an opponent who's rattled by ambient noise. So remember, it's always your choice as to how to deal with adversity. You can either grind your teeth and go ballistic, or you can glide to victory on the roar of the crowd!

THE "UNDERSTANDING LUCK" TRICK

Q: HOW CAN ANYBODY BE SO LUCKY? AND I'M NOT JUST TALKING ABOUT ONCE OR TWICE—IT'S EVERY OTHER DOGGONE SHOT!

A: Believe it or not, what most people call luck really isn't! A more accurate assessment would be, *"Somebody did just enough things right."* If you adopt that view you'll create a positive mental attitude toward everything that happens—and you'll calmly accept your opponents' fluky successes right along with your own.

So save yourself a world of grief by reciting the following mantra in any situation in which you might have previously attributed success—or the lack of it—to *luck*.

> **"THEY—OR I—DID JUST ENOUGH THINGS RIGHT. WELL DONE!"**

They just made their own luck—or you did—and that's all there is to it.

- It's *not* luck if a ball catches the net cord and then barely trickles over. It trickles over because the striker—or is that the stinker—did enough things right!

- It's *not* luck if a ball clips the net and hops over your racket, robbing you of an easy volley. You know they didn't mean to catch the top of the tape—but it *does* mean they did *enough things right* to get the ball over the net.

Once you embrace that wisdom, your time on court will become infinitely more positive and joyful. True luck is so rare as to be practically non-existent—and is confined solely to external events beyond either player's control. Below are a few examples of real luck: Good or bad depends on which side of the net you're on!

- A hawk swoops down and grabs the ball in mid flight.
- The net collapses for no apparent reason.
- Lightning strikes on a clear day.
- An incredible gust of wind comes up *completely out of nowhere.*
- A gardener starts up a leaf blower behind you while you're in mid stroke.
- A stray ball bounces onto your court.

Under any of those circumstances, you might need to replay a point that was already money in the bank. But those are the only types of situations in which luck truly plays a role. *If nothing like that happened, don't even think about bringing up the word luck!* It's just an easy out—a psychological refuge for losers and quitters.

The champion's mentality, on the other hand, is to accept the fact that no matter how random or bizarre the occurrence, 99 percent of the time somebody did just enough things right. So whether you benefited or ended up on the short end of the stick, think like a champion. Just say your mantra and get on with it: "Somebody did enough things right. *Somebody made their own luck!*"

THE "AIR CONDITIONER" TRICK

Q: SOMETIMES I PANIC DURING A TOUGH POINT. WHAT'S THE SECRET TO STAYING COOL UNDER PRESSURE?

A: The best way to stay cool is to just play *the ball* rather than your opponent! Keep your eye on the ball—just as you would with a ball machine—and forget about everything except the shot you intend to hit.

During the course of a tough point, numerous episodes can bring you right to the edge of panic. Depending on how things unfold, you might have to lunge, plunge, change direction, or even pick your racket up off the ground. Anything can happen out there—and it often does!

Those are precisely the moments when you need to keep cool. Forces beyond your control may be turning up the heat, but that doesn't mean you have to sweat it!

- Even when there's chaos all around you, *you can still turn your air conditioner up to MAX by focusing exclusively on the ball.*

Remember: No matter how hot things get, you're the one with complete control of that air conditioner thermostat—*so work it!* Just play the ball rather than your opponent, and go for your shot. It's a great way to stay cool *and* ice your opponent—all at the same time!

THE "BE PREPARED" TRICK

Q: SURPRISES SURPRISE ME! HOW CAN I HANDLE THEM BETTER?

A: Stay alert—because there's no way to avoid getting caught by surprise! Here's what you need to do when it happens:

1. Decide instantly what shot you want to play, and go with that gut reaction.
2. *If you have the necessary time,* change to the best grip for that shot.

Setting the right grip can be a lifesaver. Let's say you have to go tearing up to the net for your opponent's skillfully executed (or pathetically lucky!) drop shot.

- On your way to the ball, set your grip as quickly as possible for the shot you intend to hit, so you can put all your focus on direction when you get there. If the ball is low and about to bounce twice, Continental grip can help: It makes it easy to lead with the bottom edge of your racket to generate lift.

Then, once you've made a decision and set your grip, remember the most basic of all basics:

- *Do whatever it takes to get the ball over the net!* Even if your opponent gets to it, that doesn't necessarily mean you'll lose the point. It just means the point *might* continue for at least one more shot.

So no matter what the surprise, just pick a shot and (if possible) set your grip as quickly as you can. That's how you'll earn your "Be Prepared" Merit Badge—and once you've got it, you can start surprising your opponents for a change!

THE "COBRA" TRICK

Q: I LET WAY TOO MANY BALLS GO BY ME AT THE NET IN DOUBLES—AND BY THE TIME I DECIDE TO ACT IT'S TOO LATE. HOW CAN I GET MY MOTOR GOING UP THERE?

A: Keep your weight on the balls of your feet when you're waiting in ready position, and also after each check step (split step).

There was a popular song in the 1960s about the classic Ford Cobra sports car. The chorus goes:

> *"Spring little Cobra, getting ready to strike,*
> *Spring little Cobra with all of your might."*

Here's how to use that mindset to play your most proactive tennis around the net.

- As soon as your partner's serve or shot lands in the court, rev your motor by lifting your heels a fraction of an inch off the court to shift your weight onto the balls of your feet.

Ideally, you will have had a chance to take a little check step or hop first. But regardless, lift your heels and get ready to burn rubber in whatever direction you expect your opponent's shot to go.

You might already have a pretty good suspicion based on what they've shown you previously. If so, focus on that possibility and actually wish for them to hit it there. You'll know if your wish came true the second the ball leaves their strings.

- If it *is* an attackable ball, you'll be all primed and ready—just pop that clutch and pounce all over it! If it's not attackable, bide your time and let your partner take it.

But do stay alert for your very next opportunity to spring. In doubles, being proactive certainly doesn't imply that you try to take every ball—but it does imply that you're *ready and desirous to take every ball!*

So remember: You're a Cobra at the starting line, just waiting for the light to turn green. If you keep thinking that way, nothing that deserves to get pounced on will ever get by you again!

THE "DO IT NOW" TRICK

Q: I SOMETIMES TIGHTEN UP AND REACT MORE SLOWLY AS PLAY STARTS TO SPEED UP. OK . . . I'VE EVEN BEEN KNOWN TO FREEZE UP ONCE OR TWICE! CAN YOU QUICK THAW ME?

A: The quick thaw cure is to always do *something* right away—as soon as the ball leaves your opponent's strings!

Picture this: A genie has gifted you with a powerful magic phrase: "Slow down, sesame"—or as Popeye would say, "Slow down, sez me!"

- Now, whenever you speak that magic phrase, time instantly slows to half speed. But amazingly, only your opponent and the ball go into slow motion—while *you* stay as speedy as ever, with all the time in the world to play your shot.

Boy, oh, boy! Wouldn't that be great? But in real life it's only a fun fantasy. Luckily, the "Do It Now" trick is the next best thing.

- In the phrase "Do it now," the word "it" is your personal codeword for "Something/Anything!"
  - You need to do something—anything(!)—*as soon as the ball leaves your opponent's strings.*

So the codeword "it" could mean: Move your feet, move your racket, start running, or turn your body. Your opponent's shot is the final determinator of the first reaction you should make. But the more play speeds up, the more imperative it becomes that you do "Something/Anything" right away!

- A quick initial reaction (QIR) is always beneficial, because it gives you that much more time for vital decisions regarding shot selection and tactics. Your mind is your greatest weapon out there—and the more time you have to use it the better off you are. And no matter what anybody says, that's our story and we're sticking to it!

So always remember to "Do *It* Now!" Short of a genie in a bottle, it's the best way to make time slow down so you can avoid debilitating freeze-ups.

THE "ERASER" TRICK – Part 1

Q: ONCE I START MISSING A SHOT, IT'S ALL OVER! HOW CAN I NIP THAT IN THE BUD?

A: Erase the error immediately by modeling the correction. Short-term muscle memory is what's killing you—but it's also the key to breaking the cycle.

- *That's because whatever your muscles did last is what they'll try to do next!*

So unless you erase a funky miss, you're probably headed downhill fast—and chances are you'll continue cloning that error until you take the time to erase the blackboard.

- The most effective way to erase it is to model the stroke you meant to hit—*exactly the way you meant to hit it.*

Every stroke imprints a pattern in your short-term muscle memory, and each repetition embeds it more deeply. That's why *positive modeling,* with its dual benefit, is so important after an error.

1. First, it purges the muscle memory associated with the error.
2. Then, it overwrites that old muscle memory with a new one.

Keep in mind that for best results, you need to model your correction as soon as you can after the error. Therefore:

- Do *not* stop to swat the ball you just volleyed into the net!
- Do *not* stop to make a disgusted face!
- Do *not* stop to look up at the sun so everyone knows *why* you missed that shot!
- Do *not* stop to think of your most creative excuse ever!

Model the correction immediately, and erase the faulty data by inputting the correct information.

Granted, modeling can't give you a brand new slate, nor is it intended to. That kind of deep change takes hours of practice and many repetitions. But the power of modeling will, in an important way, at least wipe down the blackboard after each error. In Part 2 of this trick we'll look at some specific ways to maximize the benefits.

THE "ERASER" TRICK – Part 2

Q: HOW CAN I GET THE MOST OUT OF MODELING?

A: There are three different ways you can model for your next shot, depending on the improvement you want to effect.

1. IF YOU MISS A SHOT AT A CERTAIN HEIGHT AND WANT TO PREPARE FOR ITS EVIL TWIN, MODEL YOUR CORRECTION AT THAT SPECIFIC HEIGHT.

Example: If it was a low ball, model your correction down there—and if it was up at eye level, model up there. That will help ensure that your corrected muscle memory is in place and ready the next time you get a ball at that height.

2. IF YOU BELIEVE YOU SHOULD HAVE MADE CONTACT AT A *DIFFERENT* HEIGHT OR DISTANCE, MODEL THERE.

Example: If you believe you should have struck the ball further in front of you, then model your contact out there. If a lower or higher contact point would have been better, then model the correction at the strike-height you intend to use next time.

In either case, always track an imaginary ball in your mind's eye while you model. Otherwise, you'll imprint your subconscious with the idea that it's OK *not* to watch the ball—which is definitely not the case.

That leads us directly to the third way to utilize the power of modeling:

3. IF YOU MISSED YOUR SHOT BECAUSE YOU DIDN'T WATCH THE BALL CAREFULLY ENOUGH, THEN YOU NEED TO MODEL THE PHYSICAL ACT OF WATCHING THE BALL!

Here's a great way to reprogram your eye and neck muscles toward that end:

- Model the entire stroke as per usual, *but place 90% of your focus on the watching the ball part.* Start by looking forward just as you always do—and then track that imaginary ball *all the way to your desired point of contact!* That will put you right back on track with your ball watching.

There you have it: Whatever the problem may have been, one of those three types of modeling will re-program your muscle memory for future success. So choose/use the one that best fills the bill—and tap into the awesome power of modeling!

THE "EYE SEE YOU" TRICK

Q: HOW CAN I TAKE BETTER ADVANTAGE OF MY OPPORTUNITIES AFTER I HIT A GOOD SHOT?

A: Assign yourself these two trigger references:

1. Whenever you *strike* the ball effectively, stay alert for a possible pay-off.
2. Whenever you *locate* the ball effectively, stay alert for a possible payoff!

Poor recognition that you've hit an effective shot can ruin your chances of taking full advantage, because you can lose a fraction of a second (or more!) just spectating.

- The solution is to maintain a positive expectation when you hit your shots, and to pay close attention to what's going on across the net.

Watch your opponent for visual cues: Maybe they had their weight on the wrong foot, or perhaps your shot was even better than you intended! By watching for those cues, you'll quickly learn to spot instances when the tide shifts unexpectedly in your favor.

Here are some familiar examples:

- Your opponent has to run a mile for the ball.
- You see them get off to a slow start after you hit your shot.
- You expect they'll have to scoop up a low ball that's about to bounce twice.
- You just mishit your shot, inadvertently putting some weird spin on it.

See the pattern? The "Eye See You" trick is all about quickly recognizing potential problems your opponent might have with their next shot.

So whenever you think they might be in a little trouble, take a check step right before they make contact and stay mentally prepared to take advantage of the opportunity. Try it; you'll like it—and you'll be truly amazed at what you can see just by looking!

THE "I KNEW YOU WERE GOING TO DO THAT" TRICK

Q: MY OPPONENT IS PRETTY DOGGONE CLEVER, AND I'M TIRED OF GETTING FOOLED OUT THERE. WHAT'S MY BEST COUNTERMEASURE?

A: You can substantially minimize the damage they're doing by paying close attention to their preferences.

Although at first glance clever players appear to be masters of improvisation, in reality, they're often creatures of habit—albeit very sly ones! Most of them have very distinct preferences—and your job is to use that against them.

- For instance, they might love hitting a drop shot when they get a short ball to their backhand—but *never even try one* from their forehand side.
- They may only try certain shots from certain areas of the court. So make a mental note of where they are when they spring their traps.
- Also, watch out for any tricky combination they might be using, such as bringing you in with a drop shot and then lobbing over you.

Anticipation is golden against a tricky player—and the closer attention you pay to their tendencies the better off you'll be. Remember: Whatever they did last to surprise you is what they'll probably do next—*especially if it was successful!*

But forewarned is forearmed—and once you're on guard, even their cleverest tricks will be a lot less effective. So track those trends. Then, each time you win one of those points you can smile and say to yourself, "I *knew* you were going to do that!"

THE "INDY 500" TRICK

Q: WHICH IS MORE IMPORTANT—MY OFFENSE OR MY DEFENSE?

A: The truth is you can build a winning game around either one—so long as you can make a decent transition between them.

Tennis—like fencing, chess, and boxing—is a fascinating test of both offensive and defensive capabilities.

- Generally, you're on offense when you're in position to play proactively, and on defense in a reactive situation. Your location on court is not the determining factor; you can play in either mode from just about anywhere.

That's all pretty straightforward—but what makes things tricky is that the dynamics of a point often change in a flash. All it takes is one great shot by your opponent to wrest away any offensive control you might have had—and even a let cord or mishit can put you squarely (and suddenly) on defense.

- If two players are fairly evenly matched, the outcome will likely be determined by their ability to navigate those sudden transitions.

Athleticism is certainly a plus in the equation, but it's no substitute for adaptability. Think about how Indy 500 racecar drivers handle their constantly changing circumstances. Their ability to continually shift gears as necessary is a huge part of their success—and your success depends on maintaining a similarly fluid mindset.

- So when you're on offense, go pedal to the metal and attack the straightaways in high gear. But stay poised: In a nanosecond you might need to shift gears to defense—and then shift right back to offense again.

But that won't be a problem as long as you keep your mental gearbox well oiled with the realistic awareness that *anything can happen at any time.*

So start by fastening the seatbelt of positive expectation. Then, motor up in whatever style you tend to favor, watch the road, and head for that checkered flag!

THE "IDEAL PICTURE" TRICK

Q: HOW CAN I KEEP FROM GETTING DOWN ON MYSELF AFTER I MISS AN EASY SHOT?

A: The best way to eliminate toxic thoughts is to proactively replace them with clear, positive images.

As we all know, nothing is more counter-productive than beating yourself up when things go wrong. So if you sense you're headed down that slippery slope, take control of the situation and apply the brakes with this trick.

- When you miss an easy shot, take a second to picture the *exact result* you would have liked to achieve.
  - Then, replay that video in slow motion—*and clearly see yourself achieving your desired result.*

Take your time and do a good job with it, because the more detailed your visualization is, the more effectively it will purge any conscious or sub-conscious toxins.

So rather than getting down on yourself when things aren't going your way, consciously replace any toxic thoughts with vibrant, positive images. Remember, nothing breeds success like success—and if it takes a virtual reality video to get the ball rolling, go for it! Then, when a similar challenge arises, there'll be no lingering negatives to keep your *ideal picture* from becoming an ideal reality!

THE "PRETEND" TRICK

Q: I CAN TELL IT'S GOING TO BE ONE OF THOSE DAYS. PLEASE MAKE IT ALL GO AWAY!

A: If you're having an unusually sub-par day, take a deep breath and *pretend you're having an outstanding one!*

It's a fact of life that on certain days everything seems to be off—and when that happens, sometimes the only cure is magic! The "Pretend" trick is a great example; it's a simple, powerful way to achieve an amazing result.

So on days when you're really struggling with your game:

- If your forehand is way off, *pretend* you're having a fantastic forehand day.
- If you realize you aren't moving well, *pretend* you're moving like a cat!

You get the picture: Apply that "Pretend Therapy" to any area of your game that needs a critical fix.

- When you do that you create a clear and vibrant mental image of successful execution—and in response, your subconscious contributes everything in its power to mirror that in the physical world.

So harness the creative energy of your mind to manifest the reality you desire. Scientific studies have proven that the human brains can't really distinguish between an imagined event and one that actually happened, because the inner experience is the same for both. The bottom line is that your beliefs are so powerful, sometimes a little pretending is all you need to get right back on track—and change a day you'd love to forget into an affair to remember!

THE "PREPARE TO RELAX" TRICK

Q: WHAT CAN I DO RIGHT FROM THE START OF A MATCH TO HELP MAINTAIN A RELAXED STATE OF MIND?

A: Remind yourself that from the moment you set foot on court, you need to *prepare* to relax! Just as soft music and lighting set the mood for a relaxed, romantic dinner, early racket preparation sets the mood for relaxed play.

- There's no getting around it: The more slowly you prepare for a shot, the less time you have to get your ducks in a row—and the more stress you're likely to feel.

So be cool, cats and kitties: When it comes to maintaining a relaxed state of mind, early racket preparation is golden. The sooner you get started with that action, the sooner you can shift your focus toward shot selection and execution. So stay vigilant and *prepare to relax*—and stress out your opponents instead of yourself!

THE "READ MY LIPS" TRICK

Q: SOMETIMES I'M INDECISIVE IN MY SHOT SELECTION. IS THERE A TRICK FOR THAT TOO?

A: You bet. The trick is to silently state your intention for every shot prior to actually hitting it.

When you're indecisive it usually means you're in a reactive mode and you're letting the ball play you—and the best way to preempt that is to consciously state your intention for each and every shot. So the first time you practice this you'll want to do it as a drill with a hitting partner or a ball machine, because you'll want to shout your intentions right out loud.

There are four rules for this drill:

1. You must call the shot you intend to play *loudly enough for your hitting partner to hear you.* If you don't, you automatically lose the point.
2. You must call your groundies before the ball lands on your side of the court, and you must call your volleys and overheads before your strings touch the ball.
3. You must call whether you're going to hit topspin or underspin, and where you're going with your shot. For example, call out, "Underspin, down the line" or "Topspin lob, crosscourt." If you call a drop shot, underspin is understood.
4. Last but not least, remember that you *must* hit the shot you call—*or you automatically lose the point!*

It's that simple—and if you're competitive and hate losing points, you'll be amazed at how proactive you'll become in less than sixty seconds. Stating your intentions aloud in practice keeps you razor sharp mentally, and builds superb decision-making skills that benefit your entire game.

The nonpareil boxing champion Sugar Ray Robinson summed it up beautifully when he said, "Plan your work, and then work your plan." That's what the "Read My Lips" trick is all about: First declare it—and then make it happen. *Say* what you mean, and *mean what you say!*

THE "READY MIND" TRICK

Q: I'M NOT MUCH OF A POACHER IN DOUBLES, AND SOMETIMES I SPACE OUT AT THE NET. HOW CAN I STAY ALERT SO I'M READY WHEN THE BALL *DOES* COME TO ME?

A: All you have to do is imagine that without fail, *every single ball is going to come screaming right at you!* Remember, surprises abound in doubles—so use this trick 100 percent of the time.

Alertness, more than anything, is a function of expectation and desire—and no shot can catch you by surprise if you're truly expecting it to come your way. So build a strong, positive expectation habit with this phrase:

- "The only time I will ever be surprised is when the ball *doesn't come to me!*"
    - That declaration will produce a profound shift in your outlook—and soon, rather than being surprised by shots, you'll be itching for the ball to come to you!

Baseball great Yogi Berra put it perfectly: "Ninety percent of this game is mental; the other half is physical." Well, you know what he meant. So gain an edge by expecting every ball to come to you in doubles. When you do that, you'll play with a heightened level of alertness and purpose that will enhance not only your net play, but every other part of your game as well!

THE "STRINGS TO THE BALL" TRICK

Q: I OFTEN HIT LATE, EVEN WHEN I'M READY IN TIME. WHAT I NEED IS A TRICK TO HELP ME PULL THE TRIGGER SOONER.

A: If you're truly getting ready in time, all you need now is a verbal cue to spur you into action. "Strings to the ball" is a perfect proactivity phrase to get you going.

- On groundstrokes, say those words to yourself *before the ball bounces on your side of the court.* Then, just focus on moving your racket forward into the ball.
- On volleys, say those words by the time the ball is halfway to you.

Speaking, *or even thinking* the phrase "Strings to the ball" is a great dynamic catalyst. It's such a proactive instruction that it will tend to override whatever's impeding you—and that will free you up mentally and physically for a nice early strike.

So use this one anytime you're having trouble letting your shots go. Remember, "He who hesitates is lost"—so take your best game to your opponent *by proactively taking your strings to the ball!*

THE "UN-JOLT ME" TRICK

Q: SOMETIMES CAFFEINE SEEMS TO HELP ME PLAY AWESOME TENNIS—BUT OTHER TIMES IT SEEMS TO REALLY MESS ME UP. CAN I TAME THAT TIGER?

A: Sadly for all of us caffeine lovers, the answer is no.

During the Cola Wars of the 1990s, Jolt Cola ran a really cute series of ads touting their competitive edge. The ads read, "Jolt Cola: All the sugar—*twice the caffeine!*" Underneath was a picture of a wacked-out guy with his eyes spinning and his hair on end. It was very, very funny! Rather than making a lame attempt to be politically correct and health conscious, they opted for the bold approach of laying it all right on the line. You gotta love it—but that doesn't mean you gotta *drink it!*

- Let's be realistic about caffeine. If you're completely exhausted and desperately need a stimulant, caffeine *can* jump-start you physically and mentally. But overall, the disadvantages outweigh the euphoric upside. Unfortunately, caffeine has one very insidious side effect: It wrecks your ability to focus and concentrate!

A caffeinated mind is a naughty dog indeed: It'll yank your chain toward every peripheral sight or sound, and do it with bad intentions.

- That's because caffeine dramatically lowers your tolerance of minor annoyances. A bird passing overhead can distract you as much as a low flying helicopter—and a gently falling leaf can push you right over the brink. I mean, "The nerve of it. *I'm playing tennis here!!!*"

Sure, the initial lift can be mighty nice. But as euphoria morphs to frayed nerves things can get ugly fast—and just about anything that happens is likely to *really* tick you off. So if caffeine whacks you out even a little bit, use the "Un-Jolt Me" trick and *"Just say no!"* There'll be time enough to celebrate over a triple espresso *after* you've won the match!

Part VI

El Combo Grande

Combine Everything You Know—And Everything You're Capable Of Doing—In The Most Effective Way

11
STRATEGY MAGIC

QUESTIONS	TRICKS	
Will you refresh me on the difference between strategy and tactics? I think I might have cut class that day.	*Understanding & Applying Strategy And Tactics*	222
What should I do when my good stuff isn't working?	*Plan B*	223
They're killing me with their favorite shot! What can I do about that?	*Robin Hood*	224
My game is only "OK" today—fairly decent, but definitely not great. Am I better off attacking or defending?	*Bull Market*	225
I know I need to change the flow of the match, but I'm not quite sure how to go about it. So what's my first move?	*Knowing What Not To Do*	226

I'm hitting my favorite shot like a champ—and I'm still getting killed! What now?	*Hooker*	227
Sometimes I get things all set up and then I blow it! How can I clean that up?	*Risk vs. Reward*	230
It's crunch time! What should my main defensive priority be on this really big point?	*Guardsman*	231
My opponent and I are very evenly matched. What's my best game plan?	*Guess Who's Coming To Dinner*	232
My opponent is definitely better than I am. How can I possibly win?	*Underdog*	233
I can defend successfully for a while, but eventually I start wearing down. How can I get out from under that rock?	*Advanced Defensive Strategy*	234
When is the one time I should always let my opponent dictate play?	*Be My Guest*	235
I haven't won a single game yet, and I'm about to get bageled! What's the best way to launch my comeback?	*Hero*	236
I'm way too tricky for my own good. How can I stop outsmarting myself?	*Kiss*	237

What's the most important strategic concept in singles?	*Real Estate*	238
I have a really weak backhand (or forehand). Is it smart for me to shade way over in that direction so I can use my stronger stroke more often?	*Prove It*	239

UNDERSTANDING & APPLYING STRATEGY AND TACTICS

Q: WILL YOU REFRESH ME ON THE DIFFERENCE BETWEEN STRATEGY AND TACTICS? I THINK I MIGHT HAVE CUT CLASS THAT DAY.

A: Well, hopefully it was a beach day. OK, let's review:

- A strategy is *an overall plan* for achieving your desired result.
- A tactic is a *specific action* you use to implement your strategy.

STRATEGY

There are four different levels of understanding for any given strategy:

1. I've heard of it!
2. I know what it is and could explain it to a junior.
3. I understand it well enough to use it in a game.
4. I never fail to seize the opportunity to use it—*or fail to notice when it's used against me!* And I rarely, if ever, make a bad decision based on it.

I suspect we're all OK at number one—but we aren't all at number four yet! Three is a fair goal for an intermediate player; for an advanced player, four is the mandatory level of mastery.

TACTICS

Once you decide on a strategy (overall plan) for accomplishing your goal, the next step is to choose and apply an appropriate tactic.

For instance, if you're playing a woefully out of shape opponent, a good strategy would be to tire them out as quickly as possible. Now, obviously, there are several ways you can do that—each of which is a specific tactic. Two that come immediately to mind are:

1. You can run them mercilessly from side to side with wide-angled shots.
2. You can use the old "Drop-shot–Lob" combination at every opportunity.

Either of those tactics should do the job beautifully, so it's really just a matter of choosing the one that's best suited to your individual skills and abilities.

So remember: Your strategy is your canvas, and your tactics are the colors you use to paint your masterpiece. Together, they're magic—and the way you choose to use them in combination is what reveals your unique personality as a player. So mix, match and explore. Pick a strategy and a tactic, and let your creativity soar!

THE "PLAN B" TRICK

Q: WHAT SHOULD I DO WHEN MY GOOD STUFF ISN'T WORKING?

A: Don't be stubborn. Go to Plan B—*any* Plan B!

If you're like most players, there's some style you're particularly fond of—one that you like to think of as *your game*. There's a comfort level there which makes it a solid foundation on which to base your Plan A. And let's face it—anytime you can impose your will on your opponent simply by playing your game, life's a bowl of cherries.

But unfortunately, it's not always that simple. Everyone has days when they're off kilter physically, mentally or emotionally—and even if you're at the top of your game, there's no guarantee Plan A is going to work. Sometimes your opponent will have more than enough will and/or skill to rise to the challenge—regardless of how well you play.

So if your good stuff isn't getting the job done, you have two alternatives:

- You can either keep knocking on a closed door—and run the risk of a catastrophic frustration meltdown—or you can straighten your strings and move to Plan B.

Obviously, having a well-reasoned Plan B fully in mind is ideal. But sometimes, the most important action you can take is to just *make a change right now*—rather than wait until you can decide on a "perfect" adjustment. Remember:

- When Plan A appears to be a losing proposition, *any change* you make is better than *no change!*

If you're fuzzy on exactly what tack to take, clarify your options by asking two questions:

1. Which of my opponent's *strengths* do I most need to neutralize?
2. Which of their *weaknesses* can I most easily exploit?

Those answers will point you toward a constructive, proactive alternative to just continuing to plow ahead with your ineffective Plan A. Sure, it can be intimidating to leave the security of your comfort zone; but remember—bravery is doing it in spite of the fear!

So buck up and go for it: Give Plan B a shot while you're still in the thick of it, and if that doesn't pan out move right on along to Plan C. The great Bill Tilden summed it up perfectly: "Never change a winning game, but *always* change a losing game!"

THE "ROBIN HOOD" TRICK

Q: THEY'RE KILLING ME WITH THEIR FAVORITE SHOT! WHAT CAN I DO ABOUT THAT?

A: Lots of players have a tough favorite weapon—but few can wreak the same havoc with their "next best." So if your opponent is getting rich with their "A" shot and you're getting poor in the score, it's time to pull a Robin Hood.

- What's that, you ask? It's when you steal their impending victory—and give it to yourself—*by taking away their favorite shot!*

There are a number of different ways you can go about that. For instance:

- You can stop giving them balls at their favorite height.
  - If they're hurting you most when your shots stay low, use extra topspin when you can to make the ball jump up at them.
  - If they're happier when the ball bounces high, use underspin to keep it low.
- You can stop giving them balls in their favorite part of the court.
  - You already know where that is—because they've been burning you over and over from there! So whenever possible, do your best to hit the ball somewhere else.
- You can reposition yourself on court—even if that means moving to a potentially tricky area.
  - If they're killing you with drop shots, move up inside the baseline—regardless of the potential risks of playing in no-man's land.

- If they're killing you with wide serves, move way out wide to cover them—maybe even wa-aaa-ay out wide.

The key is to make *any* necessary adjustment, regardless of how peculiar it might seem. If they fool you once or twice, shame on them—but if they fool you thrice, shame on you!

Now, in the unlikely event your opponent is so versatile they can switch weapons and still squash you like a grape . . . well, hats off to them! Just have fun, and learn everything you can from the experience. But most often you'll be facing a mere mortal—one who just might bungle things when forced to go to Plan B.

So use this trick early and often, and *refuse to let anyone beat you with their favorite shot.* Remember, it's perfectly legal to steal it away from them—and give it to yourself—Robin Hood style!

THE "BULL MARKET" TRICK

Q: MY GAME IS ONLY "OK" TODAY—FAIRLY DECENT, BUT DEFINITELY NOT GREAT. AM I BETTER OFF ATTACKING OR DEFENDING?

A: If you're emotionally and physically up to attacking, that's the way to go. It has to do with the true market value of a "fairly decent" shot:

- When you attack behind a fairly decent shot the outlook is bullish—and your superior court position can only help you as you continue to tighten the screws.
- When you're defending, however, a fairly decent defensive shot may not be enough to stave off a crash. That's because as your opponent's court position improves, you face two equally unappealing scenarios:
    1. You can expect a steadily diminishing return on investment on your mediocre shots.
    2. You can expect a potentially severe market downturn after a weak shot!

When you look at it that way, it doesn't take a Wall Street wizard to figure out the sweet side of the deal. So manipulate the market to your advantage: Even on days when you're only playing OK, a bullish attacking game can sometimes send your stock skyrocketing!

THE "KNOWING WHAT NOT TO DO" TRICK

Q: I KNOW I NEED TO CHANGE THE FLOW OF THE MATCH, BUT I'M NOT QUITE SURE HOW TO GO ABOUT IT. SO WHAT'S MY FIRST MOVE?

A: When in doubt, start by focusing on "What *not* to do!"

Sometimes it can take a while to figure out exactly what you need to do to change the flow of a match, but one thing's for sure—by the time you're fifteen minutes into it, you should be really clear on what not to do!

It's easy. Just ask yourself:

- *"How are they really hurting me?"*

Then, act on the answer—and stop giving them that play!

- If they're returning exceptionally well off their backhand side, *stop serving there*.
- If they're passing you every single time you come to the net, *stop coming in*.
- If they're crunching away overheads every time you lob, *stop lobbing*.
- If they're ripping a winner on every short forehand, give them *anything except a short forehand*.

In other words, whatever it is they've been feasting on, fun's over! It's time to put them on a crash diet by taking the following pledge:

- "Under no circumstances will I continue to play to their strengths or preferences. I may not have all my ducks in a row—*but I definitely know what I'm not gonna do!*"

Armed with that commitment, you can begin to turn the tide right away. So when in doubt, start by focusing on "what not to do." While that may not be the final solution, it's a great way to buy some time while you're refining your plans!

THE "HOOKER" TRICK

Q: I'M HITTING MY FAVORITE SHOT LIKE A CHAMP—AND I'M STILL GETTING KILLED! WHAT NOW?

A: Make sure you're not hooking with a hooker! Even when your favorite shot is on fire, if it's feeding your opponent's strength, *you* could be the one who winds up getting burned.

Quick: What one-on-one sport is a virtual twin of tennis? Believe it or not, it's boxing! Both are consummate tests of skill and will, and there's plenty of hitting going on. But there's a lot more than *just* hitting: Contestants in both sports must vary power, strategy and tactics as circumstances demand—all the while exhibiting courage, stamina and desire.

The similarities end, however, when it comes to margin for error. A gross error by a boxer can put them on the receiving end of a one-punch knockout—so there's a *huge* incentive to respect an opponent's strengths. But in tennis you can only get knocked out when it's match point against you, because no matter how atrocious your execution or judgment, you can only lose one point at a time.

That means you're guaranteed at least 24 points per set to impose your game on your adversary—a nice cushion, to be sure. But that's no reason to make the often fatal mistake of failing to respect your opponent's strength.

In that regard, you need to be as vigilant as the boxer, and watch out for the one trap you should avoid at all costs:

> **NEVER HOOK WITH A HOOKER!**

That axiom has deep roots in the boxing history of Philadelphia, where the local fighters are legendary for owning two things: A huge heart and a huge hook. So needless to say, *it's almost always a bad idea to trade hooks with a Philadelphia fighter!*

And how does that apply to tennis? Well, whatever your favorite tennis weapon is, that's your personal knockout hook—be it your topspin forehand, your penetrating volley, or your oh, so sneaky drop shot.

- But as good as it might be, sooner or later the day will come when you run into someone who specializes in that same shot or tactic—and might be even better at it than you are!

In that case, *do not be stubborn*—because hooking with a hooker on a tennis court is every bit as witless as in a boxing ring!

- Sure, it's possible to win that way: But it's both difficult and dangerous—and you could easily wind up absorbing even more punishment than you dish out.

A much more efficient solution is to simply reprioritize the way you're using your primary weapon.

- In other words, use your best weapon as your *secondary line of attack,* rather than your primary line of attack!

That will both reduce your liability *and* increase your effectiveness in one fell swoop—because the more selective you are in using your hook, *the more you'll gain the advantage of the element of surprise.* And just as importantly, you'll cut your odds of needlessly absorbing a good old Philadelphia licking.

As a spectator, you can usually count on a strength versus strength contest to be an explosive, exciting, affair. After all, who wouldn't jump at the chance to see prime McEnroe vs. McEnroe, or prime Tyson vs. Tyson? But as a participant, *hooking with a hooker can be a ticket to a show you don't wanna see!* So unless you're specifically in the mood for a head-butting contest, never hesitate to wise up and change up while there's still time.

(A special word to the Ladies: Don't let the boxing analogy throw you; it's not a testosterone thing. This advice applies across the board—from hit-and-giggle social tennis to fierce Ladies League doubles, where a bruise is merely a badge of honor!)

HOOKER POSTSCRIPT:
GREAT MOMENTS IN SPORTS HISTORY

An Addendum for Lovers of *The Game*

Remember David and Goliath? Well, that was the scenario that came to mind on October 30, 1974, when Muhammad Ali challenged 25-year-old George Foreman for the undisputed Heavyweight Championship of the World in Zaire, Congo. That fight, billed as the "Rumble in the Jungle," is revered in boxing history as an archetypal match-up of guile vs. brute force.

Ali, at age 32, was years past his physical prime—and possessed neither the agility nor the stamina to elude the ferocious young champ for 15 rounds. And to make matters worse, Foreman was an awe-inspiring puncher. Joe Frazier and Ken Norton were the only two men with wins over Ali; but when they subsequently faced George, their excellent punching power seemed puny in contrast, and he destroyed both of them with brutal second-round knockouts.

So rather than engage in a suicidal attempt to hook with a hooker, Ali adopted a totally different game plan—affectionately dubbed the "Rope-a-Dope." It was a tactic that called for Ali to lean passively against the ropes and block as many punches as possible, while the aggressive Foreman pummeled him with the kind of sledgehammer blows that had demolished previous foes. For three rounds the storm raged unabated; George hammering away at his apparently helpless victim, and Ali offering practically nothing in response.

Then it happened: Little by little Big George began to fade in the African heat, and simultaneously, Ali started to counter-punch—hesitantly and in brief spurts at first, and then with increasing frequency and effectiveness. Finally, in the eighth round, he capped off the incredible upset by flooring his exhausted adversary with a sizzling combination of punches. Foreman—dazed, demoralized and confused—failed to beat the ten-count. Suddenly, Ali was—against all odds—the winner by knockout and *once again* the undisputed Heavyweight Champion of the World. Years later Foreman ruefully admitted in an interview, "It was Rope-a-Dope, alright—*and I was the dope!*"

But wait—this gets even better; it's a story with *two* happy endings! Fast-forward twenty years into the future: In an equally improbable turn of events, a much older and wiser Foreman regained the Heavyweight Championship of the World via an equally stunning upset. In 1987 he emerged from a *ten-year retirement* to win a series of tune-ups—and seven years later he finally got a shot at the undefeated twenty-six year old champion, Michael Moorer.

As expected, the slick young lefty built a huge lead on points throughout the first nine rounds. But suddenly, in the tenth, the old lion roared. In the space of five seconds he landed first one, and then a second crushing right hand—putting a paralyzed Moorer flat on his back for the full ten-count. Thus, *at an astonishing forty-five years of age,* George Foreman marked the 20th anniversary of his loss to Ali by becoming the oldest man in history to win the undisputed heavyweight championship of the world.

Well, long story short—and don't say, "Too late!"—there's just no doubt about it: Life is for learning, and it's all good. So no matter what happens on court today, remember that your tennis future is bright and full of promise. It's all about enjoying the journey: Savoring every moment, and smiling as big as big George Foreman!

THE "RISK VS. REWARD" TRICK

Q: SOMETIMES I GET THINGS ALL SET UP AND THEN I BLOW IT! HOW CAN I CLEAN THAT UP?

A: Sounds like you're going for a little more than you need to on the coup de grace. Certainly, it's important to finish off points aggressively—but it's equally important to balance risk and reward.

- Consider this: Once you've achieved a meaningful advantage in a point, odds are you're probably going to win it anyway. So before you proceed with a high-risk shot, ask yourself:
  - "Will taking this chance improve my odds *significantly enough to justify the risk?*"

Here's a nifty way to quantify it: Think of a tennis point as a lottery—with a total pot of one hundred $1 tickets. As long as the point is neutral, you and your opponent(s) each own half of the pot: Fifty tickets worth fifty bucks.

- But as you gain an advantage, you earn additional tickets. So let's give you twenty more to represent a moderate edge you've earned.

That gives you seventy tickets worth seventy bucks, or 70 percent of the total. Now those are rosy odds, indeed—but maybe you're so cautious that you'd like just a few more tickets with which to cinch the deal. In that case, I have a proposition for you:

- I'll sell you five more tickets—*but they'll cost you an additional $70!*

If you just said, "Whoa, pardner . . . I'd have to be crazy to pay that much for just five more tickets," you're absolutely right!

- Sure, you would increase your advantage by five percent. But you'd also *double your risk*—from $70 to $140—for just that minimal gain!

So why raise the ante with an expensive make-or-break shot when the odds are *already* in your favor? At worst, a lower risk shot should maintain your existing advantage—and is often enough to seal the deal without jeopardizing the advantage you already have!

THE "GUARDSMAN" TRICK

Q: IT'S CRUNCH TIME! WHAT SHOULD MY MAIN DEFENSIVE PRIORITY BE ON THIS REALLY BIG POINT?

A: When push comes to shove your opponent is likely to go with their favorite shot or play. So stay alert and ready—because it's probably coming!

It goes without saying that as a general rule, the most open area of the court begs immediate concern. But on big points, most players tend to go with their preferences—so it's essential that you factor in your opponent's proven tendencies.

A Guardsman's defensive strategy is based on the following scientific observation:

- "Twice is random. Three times is a pattern!"

For instance, let's say that your opponent has hit two extremely short crosscourt returns off nice serves to their backhand.

OK . . . that *could* be intentional—but it could just as easily be random. All you can really say at that point is *it's a potential tendency.*

- But if they spring it on you a third time, case closed! It's ACA time: Time to Accept, Concede and Assume that they have both *the will and the skill* to hurt you with that pattern.

So from that moment on, your crunch time duty as a Guardsman is to stay alert and on guard against their pet play—whatever it may be. Not only is that a great way to foil your opponent on a big point; it's also a great way to make them start second-guessing themselves. Once you send them down that slippery slope, the biggest thing you'll need to guard against is breaking into too big of a smile!

THE "GUESS WHO'S COMING TO DINNER" TRICK

Q: MY OPPONENT AND I ARE VERY EVENLY MATCHED. WHAT'S MY BEST GAME PLAN?

A: Pit your best weapon against your opponent's relative weakness—and do it as often as you can.

No matter how skilled or well-rounded your opponent is, some part of their game is not as strong as the rest. That's their relative weakness—and that's your meal ticket to the Victory Café!

- Once you spot that weakness your goal is simple: Isolate it and exploit it with a match-up that favors you.

For example:

1. You might match your reliable forehand against their erratic backhand, or your reliable backhand against their erratic forehand. You've gotta love the odds in those kinds of match-ups!

2. You might pit your accuracy of shot against your opponent's inferior conditioning. That was a favorite tactic of Andre Agassi in the second half of his career: Run 'em 'til they turn green!

3. If their only relative weakness is their volley, you might need to bring them to the net with well executed drop shots to create a match-up that favors you. Otherwise, they can just hang at the baseline and do what they do best. Andy Roddick is a fine volleyer, but he would never tell you it's the very best part of his game. As good as it is, it's still a relative weakness.

The bottom line is, there's always something in your opponent's game you can pick on—even if it's just a small differential in their level of play off one side or the other. So hone in like a hungry predator: In a closely matched struggle for survival, there's no such thing as a slight edge. Any edge is a big edge!

So be relentless, and keep as much pressure on their relative weakness as you can. Remember, there are only two menu choices at the Victory Café:

- You can either *have dinner*, or you can *be dinner!*

Oh, did you hear that? I think the hostess just called your name. It was so nice chatting with you—and bon appétit!

THE "UNDERDOG" TRICK

Q: MY OPPONENT IS DEFINITELY BETTER THAN I AM. HOW CAN I POSSIBLY WIN?

A: In that case, attack at every opportunity! You'll stand a better chance in a battle of action and reaction than you will in a contest of point construction and variety.

Let's face it; sometimes the odds are really stacked against you. Your opponent might be stronger, taller, younger, faster or more skillful—or even *all* of the above—and it always seems to happen on a bad hair day.

- But wait, all is not lost . . . UNDERDOG IS HERE! He's come to even the odds, and give you the best possible chance of winning.

Underdog knows there's always a chance, and he lives by the time-honored poker axiom, "It ain't always about what cards you're dealt—sometimes it's about *how you play those cards!*"

Underdog says, "Fortune favors the brave: So refuse to fold just because they're holding a strong hand."

- Instead, raise the stakes by attacking early and often, and fight the battle on your own terms. In other words:
    - Attack your opponent *sooner* than you normally might!
    - Attack your opponent *more often* than you normally might!

Obviously, you don't want to attack in a completely reckless or ill-advised manner—but you do want to attack at *every marginally prudent opportunity!* That strategy issues a bold statement about how you intend to respond to the challenge at hand.

So embrace the adventure. Being an underdog gives you the opportunity to far exceed your own expectations—not to mention those of your friends and acquaintances! And should your courage falter, take heart from Mark Twain's pithy observation:

- "It's not the size of the dog in the fight; it's the size of the fight in the dog."

Sure, the big dog usually wins; but Underdog says, "You just never know—and that's why you have to actually play the game!"

ADVANCED DEFENSIVE STRATEGY

Q: I CAN DEFEND SUCCESSFULLY FOR A WHILE, BUT EVENTUALLY I START WEARING DOWN. HOW CAN I GET OUT FROM UNDER THAT ROCK?

A: Your best defense in that circumstance is to deprive your opponent of the attacking option altogether!

So . . . your opponent's on the attack: The pressure is mounting and things are on the verge of getting ugly. Elementary strategy asks, "How can I best defend against their *principle* line of attack?" But in advanced strategy, the question is more ambitious.

The advanced question becomes:

Q: HOW CAN I DEPRIVE MY OPPONENT OF AN ATTACKING OPTION ALTOGETHER!

A: By making it (A) futile, and (B) counterproductive.

Q: OK—HOW CAN I MAKE IT FUTILE?

A: By forcing your opponent in the course of their attack *to rely on a weaker part of their game.*

- For example: If they have a great volley—but a weak overhead—make them pay for coming to the net by lobbing them. That way, they'll have to rely on their shaky overhead smash to finish the point.

Q: I GET IT. AND HOW CAN I MAKE IT COUNTERPRODUCTIVE?

A: By being persistent and consistent with your defensive plan. That way, their failed attacks actually exacerbate their chief weakness!

- For example: Don't necessarily go for a passing shot after they fail to put away the overhead. That would only play into their volley strength.

Instead, commit to hitting additional lobs every time they hit a weak overhead—and keep right on twisting that knife until they knuckle under. Oh, my . . . Cruella DeVille would be proud of you!

So if your opponent is grinding you down with their relentless attack, take the pressure off by rendering their strategy both futile *and* counterproductive. When it comes to defense, nothing beats the fun of depriving your opponent of an attacking option altogether!

THE "BE MY GUEST" TRICK

Q: WHEN IS THE ONE TIME I SHOULD ALWAYS LET MY OPPONENT DICTATE PLAY?

A: When they're suicidally intent on beating themselves—and they're proving it shot after shot. If they're bound and determined to give it away, the polite response is, "Cool! Be my guest."

There's a Joni Mitchell lyric that sums it up beautifully: "Don't interrupt the sorrow!" They're obviously doing a wonderful job of beating themselves, and that makes your job easy. Your task list is reduced to this:

1. Don't give them any unforced errors.
2. Don't snap them out of their daze by changing to some brand new tactic!

The first trap is an obvious one; enough said! The second, however, is even more insidious—and potentially more dangerous—because once they wake up, anything can happen. So remember:

- The last thing you want to do when things are going well is interrupt your opponent's self-destructive momentum!

So if your goal is to wind up ahead in the score, resist any naughty temptation to kick them while they're down—and *do not* throw any new wrinkles at them.

- Don't serve and volley for the first time.
- Don't drop shot for the first time.
- Don't lob—or conversely, pass—for the first time.

A wise man once said, "If it ain't broke don't fix it!"—and I say, "True that!" So never shock your opponent out of their stupor while they're going down easy. Just be cool, baby: Say, "Be My Guest"—and enjoy every minute of it!

THE "HERO" TRICK

Q: I HAVEN'T WON A SINGLE GAME YET, AND I'M ABOUT TO GET BAGELED! WHAT'S THE BEST WAY TO LAUNCH MY COMEBACK?

A: All great comebacks start the very same way:

- Win a point, and then win a game!

If you're that far behind, obviously nothing you've tried has worked—not even the "Stop The Bleeding" trick in Key Concepts. So let's get busy; time's running out and there are only two options left:

1. You can wimp out and give up. (Is that you at your best? I don't think so.)
2. You can dig down deep, and find out what you're really all about. (Scary sometimes—but oh, so worth it!)

So from here on out it's not about tennis anymore; it's gut-check time, and it's about heart and desire. And even if you're destined to go down, you might as well go down in glory.

Like all journeys, a comeback begins with a single step:

- That step is to win *just one point!*

First win one, and then do it again. Now you're cooking—you're on your way to winning a game. Keep it up! You may be getting smoked, but you're not cooked yet. *So fight, fight, and fight some more*—until you finally win that game!

Sooner or later everybody has to win a match with only their fighting heart, so why not today? Deep down inside you know there's a hero/heroine just waiting to break free—and as long as you fight your hardest, they'll hoist a cup for you in Valhalla regardless of the final score. So here's to you, Hero: It's a win/win proposition, and glory awaits!

THE "KISS" TRICK

Q: I'M WAY TOO TRICKY FOR MY OWN GOOD. HOW CAN I STOP OUT-SMARTING MYSELF?

A: Just KISS. That means, "Keep It Simple, Silly!"

In the classic "Roadrunner" cartoon series, Wile E. Coyote concocted an endless series of complex schemes to capture the Roadrunner. But there was just one little hitch: Every idea he came up with was "Too clever by half."

Wile E.'s plans were wily, all right—so wily they always went wrong. He was his own worst enemy, and it sounds like you know a little more than you'd like to about that syndrome. Luckily, there's a simple cure—and I mean that literally: More often than not, *simplicity* rules!

THE SIMPLICITY AXIOM

If there are fewer elements that can go wrong, there's less chance that something *will* go wrong.

That's the power of KISS in a nutshell—and that ain't all!

- A simple physical action is easy to repeat—so it's easier to correct and refine it.
- A simple tactical intention is easy to focus on—so you can transfer most of your attention to your shot execution. If you know you want to hit all your volleys crosscourt, there's not a lot to think about.
- A simple strategic intention is easy to concentrate on. If you're committed to hitting as many balls as possible to your opponent's backhand, it's easy to stay on track with that.

Sure, you could spice things up by using a lot of variety when you hit to their backhand—and one day that might be the perfect call.

- But if the simpler plan of just plain old hitting to their backhand is working fine, then that's *today's perfect call!*

Yes, variety can be fun, but it invariably opens a whole new can of worms: You'll not only have to decide what variations of spin and speed to use on each shot, but also, *when* to use them. That might be easy to do when you're in the zone—but it's a lot trickier when you're nervous or tired.

So if you've been too clever for your own good lately, take a hint from Wile E.'s misfortune. Remember, he was plenty tricky, but all he ever got was the "Too Clever By Half" Booby Prize. So keep it simple, and KISS the past goodbye. Start with the simplest way to get the job done—and then stick with it until there's a really good reason to change. Now, how's that for tricky!

THE "REAL ESTATE" TRICK

Q: WHAT'S THE MOST IMPORTANT STRATEGIC CONCEPT IN SINGLES?

A: It's the same as in real estate: "Location, location, location!"

Basic singles strategy is ridiculously simple:

- The idea is to locate the ball as far from your opponent as you possibly can.

The further you make them run, the more off-balance they're likely to be when they get there—and the more off-balance they are, the more difficult it will be to hit a quality shot. Obviously, that's bad for them and good for you!

Locating the ball well isn't the *only* way to make things difficult for your opponent—but it's unquestionably one of the best! So never hesitate to make it priority number one. In singles, the game is all about real estate. Location is everything, and even the homeliest shot can be worth a million if it's hit to the right spot.

THE "PROVE IT" TRICK

Q: I HAVE A REALLY WEAK BACKHAND (OR FOREHAND). IS IT SMART FOR ME TO SHADE WAY OVER IN THAT DIRECTION SO I CAN USE MY STRONGER STROKE MORE OFTEN?

A: It's always smart to reposition yourself to help cover a relative weakness—but it's *not* smart to give away too much too soon.

There are three important reasons to avoid a *premature* defensive move:

1. It's an outright confession: You might as well wear a sign that says, "I'm really worried about my ability to defend this side."

2. As you shade toward one sideline you open up dangerous crosscourt attack lines for your opponent—and the further you shift, the more vulnerable you become.

3. Worst of all, you might be defending against a threat that may never actually materialize!

That's why it's important to remain calm and not overreact to your opponent's first attempt to attack a certain area. Just because they *tried* a down the line winner doesn't mean you need to start overprotecting to that side.

- First, make them prove it!
  - Before you overcompensate, make them demonstrate the ability to *effectively* hurt you with a particular line of attack. Effectively in this case means *consistently*—not just sporadically!

So be skeptical, and never make an unnecessary adjustment based on fear. Refuse to believe a threat is real until they prove it to you—and remember, showing you something just once is definitely not proof!

12
TACTICAL MAGIC

QUESTIONS	TRICKS	
My game plan isn't working, but I'm not real versatile. Should I just plow ahead, or try something different that's out of my comfort zone?	*Deep End*	243
I can't find a single chink in my opponent's armor. What now?	*Pinholes*	244
Even after I maneuver my opponent out of position, I still have trouble finishing them off. How can I start winning more of those points?	*First Baseman*	246
My whole game is slipping away really fast. What can I do to avoid a total meltdown?	*911*	247
How can I disguise my shots better? My opponents always seem to know where I'm going to hit the ball.	*Mardi Gras*	248

My opponent is all over the net like an octopus—and they've got a great overhead too. Help: I'm totally lost!	*Compass*	250
How much should I let the game score influence the way I serve?	*Smart Pitcher*	251
I'm getting the worst butt kicking of my life, and I've tried everything. What now?	*Ultimate Last Resort*	253

THE "DEEP END OF THE POOL" TRICK

Q: MY GAME PLAN ISN'T WORKING, BUT I'M NOT REAL VERSATILE. SHOULD I JUST PLOW AHEAD, OR TRY SOMETHING DIFFERENT THAT'S OUT OF MY COMFORT ZONE?

A: *Always change a losing game*—regardless of any trepidation you might feel!

As long as play conforms to your style preferences, life is good: You can just relax in your comfort zone, as safe and secure as in the shallow end of a pool. In that best-case scenario, your preferred style will drive your opponent crazy—and unless they're clever enough to make you change, you can just wade your way to victory.

But sooner or later, doing what's comfortable won't be enough. Not only might it leave your opponent completely unfazed, but it could also feed right into their strengths.

- That's when you have to pluck up your courage and discombobulate them before they can discombobulate you!

So if your comfort-zone game is getting you nowhere fast, do something fresh to shake up your opponent—even if that means swimming toward the deep end of the pool. Maybe they're the one who can't handle deep water! So put them under pressure and find out what kind of swimmer *they* are.

For example:

- Let's say you were born to hug the baseline, but you're getting killed back there.
  - Head for deep water! If it's only *slightly agonizing* for you to come to net—but it makes your opponent wish they had never been born—it's a very good trade-off indeed!
- Or maybe you're a serve-volleyer who hates to hang around the baseline. But what if your opponent is a one trick pony, whose best weapon is their uncanny ability to hit bizarre passing shots?
  - If that's how they're killing you, you'll be better off at the baseline—even though that's the deep end of the pool for you.

It all boils down to degree of discomfort—yours versus theirs—and that's why you should never let fear prevent you from heading for the deep end. You just might find, much to your surprise, that it's your opponent who feels like they're drowning out there. So swim, little duck! Experiment and be creative—and do whatever it takes to change a losing game!

THE "PINHOLES" TRICK

Q: I CAN'T FIND A SINGLE CHINK IN MY OPPONENT'S ARMOR. WHAT NOW?

A: When a player is that solid, you might stand a better chance of breaking down their confidence than of breaking down their shots. So if you can't find an effective line of attack, try giving them a steady diet of *whatever seems to annoy them most!*

- Think of it this way: Their confidence is a giant blimp—and your task is to start deflating it, one pinprick at a time!

Jim Courier worked that to perfection in a brilliant 1998 Davis Cup match. His opponent was Marat Safin of Russia, a future US and Australian Open champ who was just eighteen years old and ranked 170th in the world. Safin won the first set 6-0 in only twenty-one minutes—basically blowing the ball right through Jim—and was up 2-0 before Courier finally won a game.

- Then, out of the blue, Jim finally found the right pin! To everyone's amazement, he started hitting medium paced one-handed underspin backhands—rather than his standard, formidable two-handed topspin. Safin seemed mesmerized by the low bouncing knife shots, and repeatedly failed to use enough ramp to clear the net. (See the "Ramp" trick in Groundstroke Magic.)

The rest, as they say, is history. Little by little, Safin started to crack, and the more frustrated he became, the more he struggled. The meltdown had begun, and Jim came back to win the second set 6-4.

Realizing he had found a sore spot, he tweaked it relentlessly with pin after pin—and although he lost the third set, he rallied to easily capture the fourth. In so doing, he pushed Safin into unfamiliar territory: The dreaded fifth set.

Long story short, Jim pin-holed him good—and his 0-6, 6-4, 4-6, 6-1, 6-4 victory gave the United States a dramatic 3-2 win in the match. As great a story as that is, it's just one example of an oft-told tale with a dynamite punchline:

- "Never underestimate the benefits of annoying your opponent!"

Not only is it a great way to turn a potentially tough match-up into an easy one; sometimes it's *the only way*—and it's simply a matter of applying the right tactic.

For instance:

- If they like low balls, give them some high bouncing topspin.
- If they like ripping away at high balls, slice a few and see how they handle having to get down low.
- If they groove on pace and nice clean shots, go to the dinkiest, junkiest stuff you can conjure up!

You get the picture: Dish out whatever it is that annoys them, and then watch their physical and emotional response. When you do strike a nerve you'll often see an immediate body language cue—and that's *your cue* to get busy with *more of the same.*

The final step, of course, is to torque up the annoyance level with the "Pinhole Abundance Principle," which states:

> If one is good, two is better.
> And if ten is good, twenty is better!

Quantity rules when it comes to pinholes, and *more is definitely better!* So shower them with abundance—and keep needling that same old spot. It's really a no-brainer: The more annoyed and frustrated they become, the better it is for you!

So don't be discouraged by your opponent's early success. No matter how solid they seem, you can still use whatever variety you possess to probe for physical, mental or emotional weakness. Remember, a few pinholes in the right place can deflate almost anyone's confidence balloon—and once you find the right needle, it's pinhole party time!

THE "FIRST BASEMAN" TRICK

Q: EVEN AFTER I MANEUVER MY OPPONENT OUT OF POSITION, I STILL HAVE TROUBLE FINISHING THEM OFF. HOW CAN I START WINNING MORE OF THOSE POINTS?

A: Strike your next shot sooner—not harder!

- When you move your opponent out of court you gain a nice time advantage—and the best way to *increase* that advantage is to strike your next shot as far out in front of you as you comfortably can.

In baseball, first basemen use a similar trick all the time. Their most frequent play requires them to catch the ball—while keeping one foot on the base—before the runner arrives. So naturally, they stretch out as far as they can for the incoming throw. Reaching out like that toward the ball gives them a small but mighty time advantage—and it'll do the same for you when you've got your opponent on the run.

There are three ways you can exploit your opponent's predicament once you get them out of position:

1. You can go for a really precise placement, very close to a line. (Yes, that can work—but it's obviously risky.)
2. You can hit the ball harder. (That can work too—but again, you increase your risk of error.)
3. You can hit the ball sooner. (Now you're cookin'—you get all the benefits, with none of the cholesterol.)

So whether it's a volley or a groundstroke, think *"Sooner—not harder"*—and then contact the ball way out in front where a good first baseman would catch it. It's the safest way to give the ball a head start in the race to the open court—and the surest way to win a lot more of those points!

THE "911" TRICK

Q: MY WHOLE GAME IS SLIPPING AWAY REALLY FAST. WHAT CAN I DO TO AVOID A TOTAL MELTDOWN?

A: Ouch! One minute you're playing fine, and the next minute you're springing leaks in places you didn't even know you had holes.

- What you've got is a bad case of MUMS—AKA: "Mysterious Unexpected Meltdown Syndrome"—and your only chance is to call 911 and ask the paramedics for a *consistency transfusion* ASAP!

Because of the way tennis is scored, it's virtually impossible to win if you're giving away every other point. So if your game is caught in a meltdown spiral, the first thing you want to do is *radically reduce your number of unforced errors.*

- Your immediate short-term goal should be to reduce them to zero—and it's not as tough as you think. The following checklist will put you right on track:

  1. Aim each and every shot well within the lines.
  2. Use plenty of net clearance.
  3. Resist all temptation to go for risky, low-percentage shots.

There you have it—the ultimate Emergency Rescue prescription.

- Remember: Consistency is not just a core element of a solid game—it's also the springboard from which most successful comebacks are launched.

So program 911 into your speed-dial, and don't hesitate to call if things start getting out of hand. There's no better option available for heading off an acute attack of MUMS.

THE "MARDI GRAS" TRICK – Parts 1, 2 & 3

Q: HOW CAN I DISGUISE MY SHOTS BETTER? MY OPPONENTS ALWAYS SEEM TO KNOW WHERE I'M GOING TO HIT THE BALL.

A: Forget about subtlety when you want to mask your intentions. Think Mardi Gras instead—where big and flamboyant rules!

- The very best disguise you can ever use is a false threat that freezes your opponent—and the more visually dramatic it is, the better.

In Part 1 of this trick, you'll learn how to disguise your follow-up shot after you've already opened up the court.

In Part 2, you'll learn how to disguise your passing shots.

In Part 3, you'll learn how to disguise your drop shots.

MARDI GRAS – Part 1: "FINISHING OFF RALLIES" DISGUISE

Once you succeed in opening up the court it's time to close the show. If you prefer finishing points with your forehand, it's to your advantage to run around the short ball and set up for an inside-out shot—which for righties is out toward your right, and vice versa for lefties.

- As you set up, make no attempt to disguise your stance! Your mission is to *broadcast your threat with a strong visual,* so as to temporarily freeze your opponent. Remember, an open stance virtually screams "Inside-out!"—and that's exactly the message you want to send.

By making the threat glaringly obvious, you force a hard choice on your opponent: They have to either stay put to cover that side of the court, or take off to defend crosscourt. Now you've got them right where you want them—and you've got two great options!

1. If they honor the threat and stay home, just hit the ball sooner (further out in front of you) for an easy crosscourt (or straight ahead) kill shot. Point over, well done!

2. If they gamble and sprint to cover crosscourt, just go ahead and hit your inside out forehand—which you're already all set up for. Too bad they didn't believe you: Once again, it's point over, well done!

From then on, whenever you show them an obvious inside-out set-up they'll have to respect that threat—or else pay the price!

That's the beauty of disguise: Whenever you make your opponent hesitate, you're in the driver's seat! When they're roaming freely and anticipating well, it might take a higher risk *great* shot to hurt them. But if you can make them hesitate, you can often close the deal with a much lower-risk *good* shot.

MARDI GRAS – Part 2: PASSING SHOT DISGUISE

When your opponent has strong net position, disguise can be the make or break element of a successful passing shot. Interestingly, the fact that they're in close is a bit of a two-edged sword for them: On the one hand, they can cut off more of your passing angles; but they also have less time to react, and anything you do to make them hesitate shifts the odds in your favor.

So just as in Part 1, it's to your advantage to show them your preferred inside-out stance whenever possible. You don't *have* to use an open stance—but it's extremely persuasive in setting up your two primary options:

1. If they linger to defend against the inside out, your disguise worked as intended! Now you're free to go crosscourt (or straight ahead) with a lower risk *good* shot instead of a higher risk *great* shot.

2. If they break early to cover the crosscourt pass, then just go ahead and hit your inside out shot. Touché . . . Olé!

MARDI GRAS – Part 3: DROP SHOT DISGUISE

If your opponent is a reasonably good athlete, the effectiveness of your drop shot will almost always hinge on the element of surprise. So approach the ball aggressively—and set up with flamboyant intentionality. Forget about being casual: Your goal is to send a broad, obvious, and *false* alarm that says, "Watch out for a power drive!"

- So advance quickly to a short ball with crisp racket prep—and then show them a slightly exaggerated version of your normal drive preparation. That extra little bit of flourish should freeze them like a Popsicle ready for a good lickin'—and that's just what they're gonna get!

Remember: A good drop shot is a truly devastating weapon—and when it's decked out in its finest Mardi Gras disguise, it's drop dead gorgeous. So don't be shy—when you're ready to give them the dropper, be blatant with your disguise. Put on your best costume, and then go strut your stuff!

THE "COMPASS" TRICK

Q: MY OPPONENT IS ALL OVER THE NET LIKE AN OCTOPUS—AND THEY'VE GOT A GREAT OVERHEAD TOO. HELP: I'M TOTALLY LOST!

A: If they're *all that,* it's going to take some mighty fine shot-making to beat them. But it can be done, if you just relax and use the "Compass" trick to regain your bearings.

First, take a look at your compass:

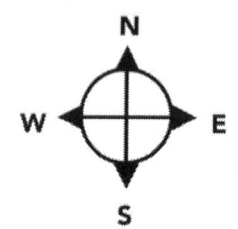

It has four cardinal points—and you have four corresponding choices when your opponent comes to the net.

Three of them are obvious, and almost everybody uses them:

OPTION 1: West – Pass to the left

OPTION 2: East – Pass to the right

OPTION 3: North – Lob up over them

But NOT everybody uses the fourth option:

OPTION 4: Go South – Drive the ball right at them!

OPTION FOUR IS A GREAT CHOICE WHEN:

- You don't like your available angles for an East or West passing shot.
- You have a short, easy sitter. In that circumstance your opponent has very little time to react, so South can be especially deadly.

That being said, a word to the wise is essential here:

> It's extremely tough to
> *consistently hit through a good volleyer—*
> and plenty of big hitters have gone down trying!

Ask anybody who had to play Sampras, McEnroe, Navratilova or Edberg. Heck, ask anybody who had to play Susie down at the local park! So be judicious, and retain the element of surprise.

Yes, playing a skilled, dedicated net-rusher can be a daunting task—but remember: *You are the compass master!* So relax and enjoy the journey. Mix it up on them regularly, and use all four points of the compass to find your way home!

THE "SMART PITCHER" TRICK

Q: HOW MUCH SHOULD I LET THE GAME SCORE INFLUENCE THE WAY I SERVE?

A: A lot! Not all points are created equal—so emulate a smart baseball pitcher, and modulate your delivery according to the count.

When a pitcher is ahead of a batter two strikes and no balls, they can throw just about any pitch they want to—and the same holds true when you're serving and you're ahead or tied in the game score.

- But when it's a crucial point which you feel you can't afford to lose, the percentage play is to make sure you get your first serve in the box.

Otherwise, you'll be in the same dicey situation as a pitcher with a full count. You'll *have* to throw a strike on the next pitch—and unfortunately, that's a fact of which your opponent will be well aware. Sure, they might let you off the hook with an error or a weak shot, but in truth you're facing a double whammy.

1. If you don't get your second serve in the box, you'll lose the point outright.
2. If it's a weak serve, they might well jump all over it.

Remember: Anytime your opponent hits a punishing return off a weak second serve, you have absolutely *no one to blame but yourself!* So take full personal responsibility, tough-love style:

- If it happens, say to yourself, "It serves me right—I deserve every bit of that!"

Then, just straighten your strings and commit to being a smarter pitcher in the future.

Your "Smart Pitcher Checklist" for big points is short and sweet:

- Focus on getting your first serve in whenever you're nervous or tight.
- Focus on getting your first serve in whenever your overall confidence level is down.
- Focus on getting your first serve in whenever you're facing a break point.

As long as you apply those simple guidelines you'll be able to enjoy the best of both worlds:

- You can be as aggressive as you like when you're even or ahead in the score.
- You can go high percentage when things are tight. It's relatively safe, and just as importantly, it will keep the pressure on your opponent where it belongs.

When it comes to serving, there's no guarantee you'll always have your best stuff—but fortunately, you *can* always pitch a smart game!

THE "ULTIMATE LAST RESORT" TRICK

Q: I'M GETTING THE WORST BUTT KICKING OF MY LIFE, AND I'VE TRIED EVERYTHING. WHAT NOW?

A: Glad you asked! This is precisely the sort of situation in which a great tennis book can single-handedly save the day. So I sincerely hope you'll have "Tennis Magic"—or something equally brilliant—right there where you can put your hands on it.

OK . . . Got it? Now here's what you need to do. (Nota Bene: Be sure to follow these instructions *exactly*. If you've *truly tried everything*, it's your only hope!)

- First, hold the book in front of you in an upright position.
- Then, reach around behind you, and carefully slide it down the back of your shorts or skirt.

Perfect! That should go a long way toward taking the edge off that spanking you're getting out there.

Oh, just one more thing . . . Don't forget to smile!

> *"Mamma said there'll be days like this,*
> *There'll be days like this, Mamma said."*
>
> ~ The Shirelles

13
JUST FOR FUN

STEVE'S PET SAYINGS

If you're as easily entertained as I am, try sprinkling in some of these sayings to enliven your lighthearted social tennis. If you do, I guarantee your pals will never forget you—no matter how hard they try!

- When someone runs a looooong way—or almost crashes into a fence trying to reach your shot—say:
  - "Alright—that's it! I'm going home if you're not gonna try!"

- When someone reacts slowly on court, ask:
  - "What is that . . . Elmer's or Super?" When they say, "What do you mean?" answer, "You know—that glue you're using on your shoes!"

- If you (or anyone else) holler, "I've got it!"—and then blow the shot, say:
  - "I *don't* got it!"

- When a relentless attacker presses in, but you successfully pass or lob them, say:
  - "Come on in—the water's fine!"

- In doubles, when you win a point after both of your opponents take a swing at your shot, say:
  - "Hey—do we get *two* points for that?"

- When you (or anyone else) is really late getting around on a shot, say:
  - "Hit that any later and it'll be _____! (Fill in an upcoming day of the week.)

- When your opponent is serving and repeatedly asks the score, say:
  - "What? Did I get here before you?"

- If you miss a shot because of ridiculously poor mechanics, try this stress buster:
  - Yell, "What was that? Nothing!!!" and flail your arms wildly.

- Whenever an opponent generously hits the ball right to you, say:
  - "Must be my magnetic personality!" (This one's even sweeter after you poach and pick off their best shot.)

- If you run a long way, only to follow up with a silly miss, shout:
  - "Come on . . . make that shot! You could have *stayed where you were* and lost that point!"

- When someone makes an atrocious error, or misses a sitting duck, or hits an incredibly lucky shot, say:
  - "I bet you can't do that with your eyes open!"

- And finally, when your tennis buddies start using all your best lines, tell 'em:
  - "Hey—write your own material!"

TENNIS MAGIC ACRONYMS

Acronyms and code phrases are powerful tools you can use to stay on track and in touch with your favorite Tennis Magic concepts. Speaking an idea aloud is a great way to initiate the all-important transformation from thought to manifestation.

Here are some of the most important:

- BIC = *Bottom Inside Corner.* For many players, BIC is the most beneficial, game enhancing trick in the book. (pg. 24)

- TTT = *Trust The Trick.* Exactly what it says: Stop relying on the rational part of your brain. Trust that the trick will work—and then work it!

- TTK = *Twist The Knife.* If you find a shot, tactic or strategy that really aggravates your opponent, *do not* stop twisting that knife. Force them to either adjust or implode. (pg. 244)

- MIB = *More Is Better.* (This is TTK's naughty twin.) If your present strategy or tactic is working well, by all means keep pouring it on. (pg. 245)

- ACE = *Anticipate – Create – Exploit*
  - Anticipate what's coming, or what needs to be done next.
  - Create opportunities.
  - Exploit weaknesses and take advantage of your opportunities.

- QIR = *Quick Initial Reaction.* This can make you or break you. (pg. 204)

- QRS = *Quick – Relax – Slow*
  - QUICK = Your quick initial reaction to the ball, as soon as it leaves your opponent's strings. That QIR can take many forms, such as turning, leaning, lunging, or saying "Oh-oh!" But whatever it is, it needs to be QUICK.
  - RELAX = The period between your QIR and the time you strike the ball. That duration might encompass lots of motion and activity if you need to sprint for the ball—but you still need to relax before you put your strings on it.
  - SLOW = The speed of the racket during the first third of the stroke. Add whatever additional speed you need during the middle third of your stroke, just prior to contact.

- BIL = *Before It Lands.* This is a sharp reminder that you want to be well into your preparation before the ball lands on your side of the court.

- BH = *Bounce/Hit:* This refers to actually saying the word bounce just as the ball bounces in your court, and then saying the word hit just as you strike the ball. It's a terrific discipline, because you have to raise your concentration to synchronize your words with the real-life timeline.

- PMA = *Positive Mental Attitude:* Maintain it at all times. (pg. 191)

- BS = *Bag Speed.* If a medium swing speed will get the job done, then stick with a medium swing speed! (pg. 38)

The next two acronyms serve double duty, in that you can use them to acknowledge both your opponent's excellence *and* your own. In either case, taking mental note of what's happening on court keeps your head in the game and helps you stay grounded.

- TMH = *Too Much Heat.* Use it as an acknowledgment that you or your opponent hit an overpowering shot. Then, back to business.

- TMP = *Too Much Pressure.* Use it as an acknowledgment that you or your opponent exerted enough physical and/or mental pressure to draw an error. Then, back to business.

And finally, two biggies that are near and dear to my heart:

- MLW = *My Little Wave.* Anytime you catch a so-called lucky break, recognize it as a pregnant moment. What it often signifies is that *your little wave* has arrived—and it's time to ride it all the way to the shore. (Surfer, pg. 190)

- ETR = *Enough Things Right.* Always stay cool and dismiss any negative thoughts when your opponent catches an apparently lucky break—because 99 percent of the time they deserve it. No matter how they won the point—or how much it hurts—you've gotta give it to them: There's no disputing that they did *enough things right!* (Understanding Luck, pg. 200)

Now you know all my favorites, but don't stop there—I strongly encourage you to create and enjoy as many fun acronyms as you can. As fond as I am of saying "Less is more," when it comes to these we're definitely talking MIB!

14
COMMENCEMENT

THE "MOJO STONE" TRICK

As your game continues to grow and unfold, I sincerely hope you'll find these tricks an enduring source of pleasure and illumination—and that within these pages you've found something you can use, something you will always remember, something that made you smile, and something that made you laugh out loud. If so, this labor of love will have accomplished all that I hoped for.

Now, to celebrate your commencement, let's tie everything together with one final bit of Tennis Magic.

It's almost game time and you're just about ready to head out—but as you're gathering your things you realize there's something missing. It's your personal Mojo Stone, the magic talisman you count on to buoy you up when the going gets rough. Whew, that was a close one—but now you've got it and you're ready for anything!

What's that, you say: You don't already own a personal Mojo Stone? Well let's get busy and fix that right now!

Because it's imaginary, you can picture it any way you like—as long as it's small enough to fit in the palm of your hand.

- So start by choosing a color you like, and then a texture. If you want it to be smooth, make it smooth—and if you want it to be rough, then rough it is. Concentrate and feel the weight in your hand, and the surface against your skin. Play and have fun with the process—and stay with it until you've created a thing of beauty.

Then, once you've created your Mojo Stone, don't leave home without it: It's your ace in the hole when all else fails. Whenever you feel like you're having a rough time on court and nothing seems to be working as it should, close your eyes and imagine you're holding it in your left hand. Then squeeze it gently; instantly, five words of wisdom will come flooding into your mind.

Those words are:

> **"THINK LIKE A BEGINNER AGAIN!"**

Always have the courage to think like a beginner. Beginners almost always limit their focus to three simple things—and you'll be amazed at what happens if you do the same!

THE BIG THREE ARE:

1. Run as hard as you can for every ball.
2. Do *anything and everything* you can to get the ball back over the net.
3. Aim the ball as far away from your opponent as you can, so they have to run a looooong way to get to it.

That's it: The Alpha and Omega of tennis, the beginning and the end. It's the best advice you can give someone who's about to play their very first point—and paradoxically, it stays golden regardless of how skillful and polished you become.

Yes, tennis *can be* somewhat more complicated—but it doesn't *have to be!* And sometimes, even the most versatile champions have had to fall back on those three basic principles in order to snatch victory from the jaws of defeat.

- So always listen to your Mojo stone when you find yourself in a deep dark hole—and dare to play like a beginner again! With this one last trick up your sleeve your training is complete, and you're forever armed and dangerous.

Therefore, in recognition of your achievement, dedication and valor, I hereby christen you a Knight Of The Realm of Tennis Magic. Continue ever onward on your quest, Lords and Ladies. I truly believe that the journey *is* the destination, and wish you a constantly joyful adventure. Now get out there on court and have big fun—and happy hitting always!

Commencement

TRICK TITLE INDEX

911	247		Cell Phone	158
A-B-C Of Tennis	37		Cobra	203
Actually	9		Collapse It	167
Advanced Defensive Strategy	234		Compass	250
			Conquistador – Pt. 1	165
Air Conditioner	201		Conquistador – Pt. 2	166
Archery	109		Deep End	243
As Above, So Below	173		Denial	122
Bag Speed	38		Desire	198
Ball Is My Friend	28		Do It Anyway	194
Batter With Two Strikes	121		Do It Now	204
Be Here Now	39		Don't Let Go	116
Be My Guest	235		Drill Sergeant	174
Be Prepared	202		Early Bird	87
Big Two, Little Two	88		Either / Or	41
Bottom Line	40		Eraser – Pt. 1	205
Breathe Easy	171		Eraser – Pt. 2	206
Brush The Crumbs Off The Table	89		Eye See You	207
			Faithful Servant	42
Bull Market	225		Fifteen Degrees	91
Cat	187		Fingernails	143
Catch It	133			

Finish It	73	Ideal Picture	210
Finish Line – AKA: Hip Trick	110	Indy 500	209
First Baseman	246	Introduction To The Volley	128
First Serve In	107	Jog It Out	169
Flashlight	157	Keys To The Castle	23
Fork In The Road	192	Kiss	237
Four Quarters – Pt. 1: "BIC It!"	24	Kissing	155
Four Quarters – Pt. 2	27	Knowing What Not To Do	226
Get My Meaning?	43	Kung Fu	141
Graph – It's Only A Blip!	191	Las Vegas	44
Grip Trick – Serve	105	Lean On Me – Pt. 1: There's A New Kid In Town	129
Grip 1 – Forehand Volley	151	Lean On Me – Pt. 2: Zip It!	130
Grip 2 – Forehand Volley Extreme	152	Lean On Me – Pt. 3: Fear Not!	132
Guardsman	231	Let It Finish	45
Guess Who's Coming To Dinner	232	Lock On Target	113
Hawk	156	Magic 44	46
Helmet	139	Make The World Stop Spinning	188
Hero	236	Mardi Gras	248
Hold That Pose	170	Megaphone	146
Hold That Wrist	144	Mighty Oak	120
Home Base	92	Millionaire	197
Hooker	227	Model It	175
I Can See Clearly Now	111	Mojo Stone	261
I Knew You Were Going To Do That	208		

Trick Title Index

My Checkered Path	35
Next.Com	49
Nose To The Ball: Serve	114
Nose To The Ball: Groundies & Volleys	168
Now I've Got You	193
Obsolete Commandment: Forehand	31
Obsolete Commandment: General Footwork	33
Palm It	101
Peter Pan	50
Pinholes	244
Plan B	223
Pot Of Gold	117
Power Leg	82
Predator	123
Prepare To Relax	211
Pretend	210
Prime Directive	51
Pro	52
Prove It	239
Ramp	70
Read My Lips	212
Ready Mind	213
Ready, Set, Go!	94
Real Estate	238
Revised Commandment: General Footwork	34
Reward & Punishment 1	196
Reward & Punishment 2	196
Rib	153
Risk vs. Reward	230
Roar Of The Crowd	199
Robin Hood	224
Sherlock Holmes	53
Shuffleboard	142
Slump Buster	108
Smart Pitcher	251
Spear – AKA: King Pete	103
Squashing Grapes	176
Squeeze	177
Sticky Foot	178
Stop And Go Find – Pt. 1	136
Stop And Go Find – Pt. 2	137
Stop The Bleeding	30
String Quartet	95
Strings To The Ball	214
Super Laser Vision	54
Surfer	190
Surrender	55
Swing Away	140
Swish	115
Target	96
Terminator	97
Tried And True	56

Turnabout	58
Ultimate Last Resort	253
Un-Jolt Me	214
Underdog	233
Understanding & Applying Strategy And Tactics	222
Understanding Luck	200
Understanding Open & Closed Stance Groundstrokes	67
Video-Cam	138
You Cannot Be Serious!	189
Zap The Boogeyman	59
Zen Mind	60
Zen Reverse-Mind	195
Zorro	147

ISBN 1-41204202-X

3260946R00151

Printed in Great Britain
by Amazon.co.uk, Ltd.,
Marston Gate.